The Continenta

A Farce

Joan Greening

Samuel French – London
New York – Sydney – Toronto – Hollywood

© 1980 BY SAMUEL FRENCH LTD

Rights of Performance by Amateurs are controlled by Samuel French Ltd, 52 Fitzroy Street, London W1P 6JR, and they, or their authorized agents, issue licences to amateurs on payment of a fee. **It is an infringement of the Copyright to give any performance or public reading of the play before the fee has been paid and the licence issued.**

The Royalty Fee indicated below is subject to contract and subject to variation at the sole discretion of Samuel French Ltd.

Basic fee for each and every
performance by amateurs   Code K
in the British Isles

The publication of this play does not imply that it is necessarily available for performance by amateurs or professionals, either in the British Isles or Overseas. Amateurs and professionals considering a production are strongly advised in their own interests to apply to the appropriate agents for consent before starting rehearsals or booking a theatre or hall.

ISBN 0 573 11057 3

Please see page iv for further copyright information

CHARACTERS

Michael Feather
Richard Feather
Gloria Grant
Marion Feather
Elizabeth Feather
Priscilla Plankton
Humbert Carpington
Julia Jones
Angela Leyton
Henry Feather

The action takes place in the lounge of Michael Feather's three-bedroomed flat

ACT I Late on a summer evening

ACT II The following morning

Time—the present

To John, with love

COPYRIGHT INFORMATION

(See also page ii)

This play is fully protected under the Copyright Laws of the British Commonwealth of Nations, the United States of America and all countries of the Berne and Universal Copyright Conventions.

All rights including Stage, Motion Picture, Radio, Television, Public Reading, and Translation into Foreign Languages, are strictly reserved.

No part of this publication may lawfully be reproduced in ANY form or by any means—photocopying, typescript, recording (including video-recording), manuscript, electronic, mechanical, or otherwise—or be transmitted or stored in a retrieval system, without prior permission.

Licences for amateur performances are issued subject to the understanding that it shall be made clear in all advertising matter that the audience will witness an amateur performance; that the names of the authors of the plays shall be included on all programmes; and that the integrity of the authors' work will be preserved.

The Royalty Fee is subject to contract and subject to variation at the sole discretion of Samuel French Ltd.

In Theatres or Halls seating Four Hundred or more the fee will be subject to negotiation.

In Territories Overseas the fee quoted above may not apply. A fee will be quoted on application to our local authorized agent, or if there is no such agent, on application to Samuel French Ltd, London.

VIDEO RECORDING OF AMATEUR PRODUCTIONS

Please note that the copyright laws governing video-recording are extremely complex and that it should not be assumed that any play may be video-recorded for whatever purpose without first obtaining the permission of the appropriate agents. The fact that a play is published by Samuel French Ltd does not indicate that video rights are available or that Samuel French Ltd controls such rights.

ACT I

The lounge of Michael Feather's flat. Late on a summer's evening

The flat is simply but comfortably furnished, with a sofa, armchair, drinks table, sofa table, and telephone table. There are doors to three bedrooms. Other doors lead to the bathroom, kitchen and the public corridor

As the CURTAIN *rises, Mike Feather, handsome, thirty-five, enters from the bathroom in pyjamas and dressing-gown, switches off the lights, and goes towards Bedroom 3. The front doorbell rings. Mike sighs, switches the lights back on, goes to the front door and opens it*

Dick Feather stands outside. He is thirty-three, and also handsome

Mike Oh no!
Dick Oh yes. Hallo, Mike
Mike Hallo, Dick. I might have known. What the hell are you doing here at this time of night?
Dick I was—er—er—just passing by.
Mike With a travelling bag?
Dick That's right, and I thought I'd pop in.
Mike In that case you'd better pop out again. I'm going to bed.
Dick Please, Mike, I've had some bad luck.
Mike So have I!
Dick Oh dear, what's happened to you?
Mike You've arrived.
Dick Mike, please let me stay here.
Mike What have you been up to this time?
Dick Well I, er . . .
Mike Another row with Marion, I suppose.
Dick Not really. It was more Marion having a row with me. She's not very pleased. She's thrown me out.
Mike What did she say?
Dick Get out.
Mike Did it work?
Dick Oh yes, I got out.
Mike I must remember that. "Get out", and he goes.
Dick No, I wouldn't if you said it. I'd know you didn't mean it. I can always rely on your intrinsic goodness, your kind nature, your family feeling. Oh, you're a wonderful brother.
Mike And you're a crawler! If you're not careful you'll end up like Father. You really do get yourself into it, don't you? You should try and lead a calm, orderly existence, like me.
Dick Please can I stay here, Mike? I can't go home to Mother again.

Mike Again?
Dick I've been there three times this month already.
Mike Oh Dick! What's happened this time?
Dick It's not my fault. For once it's really not my fault.
Mike That makes a change. What's Marion done, then?
Dick She—er—she came home too early.
Mike She came home too early? What are you talking about?
Dick She caught me out.
Mike Caught you out? Where were you, then?
Dick In the bedroom.
Mike But you said she caught you out.
Dick Yes, she did. In the bedroom with Angela Leyton.
Mike I'm ashamed of you. In the bedroom with Angela Leyton, and you say it's all Marion's fault.
Dick Well, it is. I was only showing her the new continental quilt but Marion didn't believe me.
Mike I'm not altogether surprised. I'm not sure that I believe you. And then she said "Get Out".
Dick Er—yes.
Mike Is that it?
Dick Er—no.
Mike Come on, let's have the full story.
Dick Actually, she said "Get out from under that quilt". We were only trying it out.
Mike Trying what out?
Dick The quilt.
Mike The quilt?
Dick Yes.
Mike And who is this Angela Leyton?
Dick Oh Mike—she's fantastic. She lives next door and I met her the day after we moved in. It only took one look.
Mike And a continental quilt.
Dick Oh it's all right for you. You're not married. It must be wonderful living on your own.
Mike Don't sidetrack. What are you going to do now?
Dick Stay here?
Mike O.K. Just for tonight but you'll have to sleep in the small room. I'll go and get some sheets. I don't suppose you've brought your new continental quilt with you.

Mike exits to the bathroom

Dick pours himself a drink and sits in the armchair

Gloria enters from Bedroom 3. She is twenty-two, beautiful and intelligent

Gloria Come on, darling. I've been waiting and waiting and waiting. Aren't you coming to bed? There won't be any night left.
Dick (*rising*) Er, er I think you've got the wrong man.
Gloria I wouldn't say that. A different one perhaps. Who are you?

Act I

Dick I'm Dick. Mike's brother. I'm more than pleased to meet you.
Gloria Oh, Mike never told me he had a brother.
Dick Mike never told me he had you.
Gloria Oh, he hasn't—er—had time, I mean. I only moved in today. I'm Gloria.
Dick So you're going to live here with Mike—in there?
Gloria Yes. Isn't it a lovely flat, and it gets better by the minute. What are you doing here?
Dick Mike's letting me stay here tonight. My wife's rather cross with me.
Gloria Have you been a naughty boy?
Dick No, I haven't. I didn't have time.
Gloria Tell me about it. What have you been doing?
Dick We had a disagreement about the continental quilt.
Gloria Who was getting the most you mean?
Dick Yes, something like that.
Gloria Yes, I know. I had an experience like that once.
Dick You did?
Gloria Oh yes, everytime he turned over—I found myself without.
Dick Without what?
Gloria Without any quilt.
Dick Was that the end of it?
Gloria Of course. We got blankets after that.
Dick Oh?
Gloria Where are you going to sleep?
Dick In there.
Gloria Shall I get the room ready for you?
Dick Oh no, thanks. Mike's getting the sheets.
Gloria I'll make the bed up for you. I'm very good at it.
Dick I'm sure you are.

Mike enters from the bathroom with the sheets

Mike Oh, I see you two have met.
Dick You kept this quiet, didn't you?
Mike Yes, and so will you if you know what's good for you?
Gloria Why didn't you tell me you had such a gorgeous brother? Let me take those. I'm going to help him. (*She takes the sheets and Dick by the hand*)
Mike Don't be too long or too helpful.

Gloria and Dick exit to Bedroom 1

The doorbell rings. Mike opens the front door

Marion stands there. She is thirty, and attractive

Marion! Why, hello. How are you? Nice evening, isn't it?
Marion What's the matter with you, Mike. Why don't you ask me in?
Mike Um—er—just going to bed. Not the right time to be socializing. Come back tomorrow. I'll be pleased to see you tomorrow. (*He tries to shut the door*)

Marion Will you please stop being silly and let me in. I want to talk to you.

She pushes past him, carrying a holdall

Mike Please be quick, then. I'm going to bed soon. I've just developed a shocking headache.
Marion Don't worry I've got some marvellous pills in my sponge-bag. I'll let you have one when I've unpacked.
Mike Unpacked! You can't mean you've come to stay. What's wrong with your house?
Marion That's what I want to talk to you about.
Mike Well, hurry up. My back's bad as well.
Marion Oh Mike, we've always got on well, haven't we?
Mike Ye-es.
Marion Well I want you to help me.
Mike I will if I can. What's this about?
Marion Give me a drink, will you?
Mike The usual?
Marion Yes, please.
Mike Come on, then, tell Uncle Mike all about it.
Marion Did you know Dick's got another woman?
Mike Look, Marion, Dick's my brother, family loyalty and all that.
Marion You mean you wouldn't tell me if you did know anything.
Mike Perhaps you'd better tell me your side of the story.
Marion You know we moved into our new house a week ago?
Mike Yes.
Marion The first day was marvellous, and then we met our new neighbour.
Mike New neighbour?
Marion Angela Leyton. She's a bitch and thinks any man is a personal challenge. Dick, not being very strong-willed, only had to take one look and he was won over. I had to go out tonight, and when I got back—there they were.
Mike Where?
Marion Can't you guess? And then they tried to tell me some absurd story about trying out the continental quilt.
Mike You didn't believe them?
Marion Would you have done?
Mike Well...
Marion And now he's gone to his mother's.
Mike How do you know?
Marion He always goes there when we have a row.
Mike I wish he had.
Marion What did you say?
Mike My head's very bad.
Marion I'm sorry to tell you all my troubles, but Mike—I said some dreadful things to him, and I don't know what to do.
Mike You want him back?
Marion Only if she gives him up.
Mike Is she very beautiful?

Act I 5

Marion Oh yes, she is, even if I do hate her.
Mike I still don't know quite what you're doing here.
Marion No, nor do I. Only I thought that, if I wasn't there when he got back, if he comes back, he might think I'd gone off with another man and be terribly jealous. What do you think?
Mike No good, it won't work. I think you'd better go home and think again.
Marion I'm not going home. You've got to let me stay here. Mike, I've just had a wonderful idea. What about us pretending to have an affair?
Mike Who?
Marion You and I.
Mike That's what I thought you said.
Marion Then he'd be really jealous. He's always envied you.
Mike He wouldn't envy me this.
Marion What did you say?
Mike I can't agree to this.
Marion Why not?
Mike He wouldn't like it. He'll be furious. He might try and strangle me.
Marion Exactly. That's just what I want.
Mike I don't.
Marion (*moving to the bedroom*) This is your bedroom, isn't it?
Mike Yes, but you can't go in there.
Marion Of course I can. I must get changed if we want it to look authentic.
Mike No, I refuse. It's a stupid idea. How will he know anything about it?
Marion Because you're going to get him here on some pretext.
Mike What pretext?
Marion I don't know. I can't think of everything. You're the one with all the ideas.
Mike My mind's gone blank.
Marion Sit there and think hard. I'm going to change.

Marion exits to Bedroom 3

Mike goes and pours himself a large drink and downs it in one gulp. The doorbell rings. He goes and opens the front door.

Elizabeth Feather stands there. She is a domineering woman of fifty-five. She carries a case.

Mike Mother. What are you doing here? You can't come in. I'm ill, really ill. You'll catch it. You must go home again. It might be the black plague or leprosy or yellow fever.
Elizabeth You don't look ill to me. Nothing a good dose of castor oil won't put right.
Mike Mother, why are you carrying a case?
Elizabeth Because I have come to stay.
Mike I don't believe it.
Elizabeth I knew you'd be pleased.
Mike Ecstatic.
Elizabeth I hope you haven't been drinking.

Mike Oh Mother, how could you?
Elizabeth I think it's as well I've come so I can keep an eye on you.
Mike Where's Dad?
Elizabeth I've left your father.
Mike It's not fair.
Elizabeth What did you say?
Mike Sit there.
Elizabeth Thank you, Michael. Your father is quite insufferable and I refuse to live with him any longer. I'm going to live here and look after you. You'll like that won't you? Just you and I.
Mike And all the rest.
Elizabeth I beg your pardon?
Mike Mother knows best. What has Dad done, exactly?
Elizabeth You'll find it hard to believe.
Mike Try me.
Elizabeth When I returned from my bridge club, I found him sitting in front of the television set.
Mike So?
Elizabeth There was a lewd programme on. One which I had forbidden him to watch.
Mike Is that all?
Elizabeth No, Michael, that is not all. He was enjoying it!
Mike Poor old Dad.
Elizabeth What did you say?
Mike How very bad.
Elizabeth Indeed it was.
Mike I think you should give him another chance. Why don't you go home and make it up with him?
Elizabeth I, make it up with him, when it's entirely his fault? Certainly not. You'd better get me some sheets and I'll make up my bed. Which room will be mine?
Mike (*doing quick mental calculations and then pointing to Bedroom 2*) This one, Mother.
Elizabeth I'll sleep there for tonight, but I expect you to move your things out of the large room tomorrow and I'll have that one.
Mike Yes, Mother, but you'd be more comfortable at home.
Elizabeth I'm staying.
Mike Bloody hell.
Elizabeth I beg your pardon?
Mike Oh, very well—I'll get the sheets.

Mike exits to the bathroom

The doorbell rings. Elizabeth opens the front door

Priscilla Plankton enters. She is a spinsterish woman of thirty-nine

Elizabeth Yes?
Miss Plankton Oh—er—is—er is Michael here?
Elizabeth What do you want Michael for?

Act I

Miss Plankton I want him to help me.
Elizabeth Well, he can't tonight.
Miss Plankton Isn't he here then?
Elizabeth Yes, but he's occupied.
Miss Plankton I wouldn't keep him long.
Elizabeth Who are you exactly?
Miss Plankton I'm his next-door neighbour that side.
Elizabeth Are you in the habit of calling on young men at this time of night?
Miss Plankton Oh no, only when I am desperate.
Elizabeth Desperate for what?
Miss Plankton Desperate for some help.
Elizabeth Well, can't it wait until morning?
Miss Plankton I suppose so. I've waited so long.
Elizabeth No, you haven't. You've only just arrived.
Miss Plankton Are you sure Michael can't see me?
Elizabeth Of course he can't. Unless he can see through walls. He's in the bathroom.
Miss Plankton Oh well, in that case I'd better come back later.
Elizabeth Yes, much later. In the morning preferably. I don't approve of people knocking on my son's door at this time of night.
Miss Plankton Michael is your son?
Elizabeth Of course he is.
Miss Plankton I am relieved. I thought his taste had changed?
Elizabeth His taste in what?
Miss Plankton Gir—rapes. Grapes, he likes white ones.
Elizabeth What do you mean? How has his taste changed?
Miss Plankton He used to prefer black ones.
Elizabeth He did not. I never allowed him to eat grapes as a small boy.
Miss Plankton Well, of course, I didn't know him then.
Elizabeth No, you would have been rather old to have been his playmate.
Miss Plankton I'm sure he was very nice.
Elizabeth Yes, he was as good as gold. He hasn't changed.
Miss Plankton That's all you know.
Elizabeth What did you say?
Miss Plankton I'm glad you told me so.
Elizabeth Yes, never a moment's trouble with him. And now he's grown up it's the same. He's always behaved himself in an exemplary manner. Takes after me, of course.
Miss Plankton Is he your only son?
Elizabeth Oh no, there's another, but he's a different type altogether. He's never settled down. It's a great sorrow to me.
Miss Plankton You'd like him to have a girl-friend?
Elizabeth Certainly not.
Miss Plankton You can't keep him for ever.
Elizabeth He seems to think I can.
Miss Plankton He might settle down if he had a wife.
Elizabeth Oh no, he wouldn't. He has got one, and it's made no difference. He's never with her.

Miss Plankton Where is he, then?
Elizabeth When he's not with me, he's usually here with Michael. I'm glad about that in a way because Michael sets him such a good example. He shows him the right way to do everything.
Miss Plankton Everything?
Elizabeth Yes.
Miss Plankton I suppose he's not here now?
Elizabeth No, no. I expect he's at home.
Miss Plankton I couldn't have his address, could I?
Elizabeth No, you certainly could not.
Miss Plankton It was just a thought.
Elizabeth Do you usually go round asking for the address of young men?
Miss Plankton Not usually, but I'm forty the day after tomorrow...
Elizabeth Really—you look much older.
Miss Plankton And I want to do something I've never done before—before I'm forty.
Elizabeth Well, you're not going to do it with my sons.
Miss Plankton No, no you misunderstand me. I want to say "Yes" to a proposal of marriage.
Elizabeth I'm afraid my sons can't oblige. Richard's already married and Michael would never have anything to do with a forty-year-old woman.
Miss Plankton A thirty-nine-year-old woman.
Elizabeth No, still much too old.
Miss Plankton But I don't want them to ask me, I want someone else to ask me.
Elizabeth If you've only got two days left, I suggest you go out and start searching.
Miss Plankton But I want to see Michael for advice on how to...
Elizabeth He'd tell you the same. Off you go, now.
Miss Plankton But I don't know how...
Elizabeth I don't know where you'll find anyone to propose to you at this time of night but if you'll take my advice...
Miss Plankton Yes?
Elizabeth Don't waste time here.

Elizabeth pushes Miss Plankton out of the front door. Gloria enters from Bedroom 1

And who, may I ask, are you? And what are you doing in my son's flat?
Gloria Your son's flat?
Elizabeth Yes, I'm Michael's mother. What are you doing here and dressed in that absurd way?
Gloria What do you mean. This is my new nightie. It's the new wet look.
Elizabeth It certainly looks as though you're pouring out of it. You'll catch your death of cold. Shouldn't you wear a vest under it?
Gloria A vest!
Elizabeth Yes, you should always wear a vest, no matter how warm it may seem.
Gloria What—even in bed?

Act I

Elizabeth Especially in bed.
Gloria I don't usually wear this either. I like sleeping without a stitch on. This is only to float about the place in.
Elizabeth You sleep without a stitch on?
Gloria Oh yes, it's a wonderful feeling, saves time, in the mornings too. You should try it.
Elizabeth My chest is far too delicate to risk the night air getting to it. Now, I asked you what you were doing in my son's flat, not about your immodest habits.
Gloria I'm staying here.
Elizabeth Staying here! I don't like the sound of that. I hope you're not implying what I think you're implying.
Gloria I wasn't aware that I'd implied anything. I merely said I was staying here.
Elizabeth You're not—with *my son*, are you?
Gloria Certainly not. As if I'd be interested in him.
Elizabeth What do you mean? What's the matter with Michael?
Gloria Nothing that I know of. It's just that I've got someone much better.
Elizabeth Better than my son?
Gloria Oh yes. My boy friend lives next door. I'm only staying here because it wouldn't be right to sleep in the same flat before we're married.
Elizabeth Admirable sentiments. There's far too many goings on these days. I'm glad my son leads a blameless life. He takes after me, of course.
Gloria Like hell!
Elizabeth What did you say?
Gloria Er—quite well.
Elizabeth Who is?
Gloria I am.
Elizabeth Are you?
Gloria Yes, thank you for asking!

Mike enters from the bathroom, sees Gloria and Mother and tries to exit again

It's all right, Mike. I was just explaining to your mother how my boyfriend lives next door and how you kindly said I could sleep in the spare room, and that's where I am going to sleep tonight, all night, all right?

Gloria exits to Bedroom 1

Mike Oh no.
Elizabeth What did you say?
Mike Just so.
Elizabeth Oh, by the way, a mad woman called looking for someone to propose to her.
Mike What was her name?
Elizabeth I don't know, I didn't ask her. I said that you wouldn't be interested.
Mike What was she like?
Elizabeth Old and dowdy.

Mike Quite right, Mother, I wouldn't be interested.
Elizabeth Of course you wouldn't. Exemplary life. Well, if you could give me my sheets, I'll be off to bed. I'll see you in the morning.
Mike Oh hell!
Elizabeth What did you say?
Mike Sleep well.
Elizabeth I will. Good night.

Elizabeth exits to Bedroom 2

Mike pours another drink and gulps it down

Dick opens the door of Bedroom 1

Dick Psst, psst!
Mike No, but I wish I was.
Dick Is it clear?
Mike Yes, all clear.
Dick Gloria's just told me that the old battlehorse has arrived.
Mike Yes, she charged in five minutes ago.
Dick Where is she now?
Mike In there.
Dick Does she know I'm here?
Mike Not yet.
Dick You won't tell her will you, Mike?
Mike Depends.
Dick On what?
Mike On you.
Dick Look, Mike, if she knows I've left Marion again she'll cut off the most precious thing I've got.
Mike You mean your . . .
Dick Yes, my allowance.
Mike Your allowance. But you don't need that. Last time I saw you, you said you'd got a lot of new patients.
Dick Well, I've had staff problems, and I've had to buy a new drill and you wouldn't believe how much it cost to decorate the surgery, and then there was the new reclining chair.
Mike What did you need a new reclining chair for?
Dick The old one got stuck.
Mike Got stuck. Are we still talking about the chair?
Dick Of course we are.
Mike And was there anyone in it at the time?
Dick Oh yes. That's what caused the staff problem. She said it wasn't made to take two and walked out. I've been looking for a new receptionist ever since.
Mike Surely it can't be hard to find a dental receptionist?
Dick It's very hard to find them with the right qualifications.
Mike "O" levels, you mean.
Dick Oh no, I'm not interested in "O" levels. I expect them to be willing, able, under twenty-five, very beautiful, with a modicum of intelligence.

Act I

Mike No wonder you can't find anyone. You expect too much.
Dick Oh, do you think I should waive the under twenty-five requirement?
Mike Certainly not. If something has to go it must be the modicum of intelligence.
Dick Anyway, with one thing and the reclining chair, I'm rather short at the moment.
Mike It doesn't sound to me as if you're short of anything, except brains.
Dick Thanks a lot.
Mike Now don't get moody. I'm only telling you this for your own good.
Dick You only say that when you're going to insult me.
Mike Yes, I am. You've made a dreadful mess of things, haven't you?
Dick I suppose so.
Mike It's all very well having the inclination . . .
Dick Yes, that's why I got the reclining chair . . .
Mike But you must also have the basic requirements.
Dick Oh, I've got those.
Mike I mean you must have talent, attraction, efficiency, good organization, and be a damned good liar.
Dick (*counting them on his fingers*) I'm quite attractive, aren't I?
Mike Not to me I'm pleased to say. Now you must try and learn from me, Dick. You must watch and see how I do things until you get some ideas of your own, and until you have, you must crib mine.
Dick Well, I'll try.
Mike I should never have got myself in your position but if I had I'd never have said anything so absurd as "we're only trying out the continental quilt". As if anyone would believe that. I should have immediately used my brain power, my enormous resources and come up with a brilliant explanation that everyone would believe.
Dick Oh, what would you have said?

Mike opens, then shuts his mouth

Mike There you are side-tracking again. It's not me we're talking about, it's you.
Dick I was only trying to learn from you.
Mike That's the idea. Now then, remember, quick thinking is what's needed if you're going to get out of this one.
Dick You've always been more successful, haven't you?
Mike Oh, I wouldn't say that.
Dick I would.
Mike No, you did quite well with that—er—what was her name? Ah yes Jessica Gooch. Difficult to forget a name like that.
Dick Yes.
Mike I seem to remember she was potty about you. Didn't she bombard you with phone calls and letters?
Dick Yes.
Mike And didn't she come round one day and refuse to go home until you'd promised to go out with her the next day?
Dick Mike, I was only six at the time.

Mike A success is a success no matter how young. And then there was that—er—Janis Jefferies. Do you remember her?
Dick Yes.
Mike Wasn't she the one with the big...
Dick Brother. I still have the scars.
Mike And then, there was that little girl in the second form, Monica, that was it, who kept enticing you into the park.
Dick Yes.
Mike Did you go?
Dick Yes.
Mike Well, what happened?
Dick Nothing.
Mike Well, why not?
Dick I fell into the duckpond.
Mike How on earth did you manage that?
Dick I was pushed.
Mike Who by?
Dick Monica. That's why she kept enticing me into the park.
Mike (*laughing*) I wish I'd seen it.
Dick I might have known you'd find it funny. I could have caught something *really* nasty.
Mike What did you catch, then?
Dick A clip round the ear from Mother for getting my clothes wet.
Mike Talking of Mother, I think we'd better break up these romantic memories in case she catches you and gives you another clip round the ear.
Dick You mean you won't tell her I'm here?
Mike I won't on one condition.
Dick Yes?
Mike That you return Gloria in perfect condition.
Dick I will try and soothe her down for you but she's very upset because Mother called her immodest. But I'll do my best to return her to your room untouched by human hand.
Mike My room. Oh no, don't do that. Mother will be next door. You'd better keep her with you after all. You can sleep on the floor.
Dick If you insist I'll do my best to keep her with me, but I can't promise to sleep on the floor.
Mike Mother. Allowance.
Dick I'll sleep on the floor.
Mike That's one thing settled.
Dick What's the matter? You look all in.
Mike That's just what I am. All in the...

The doorbell rings

Oh no, who can that possibly be? Look, get back in your room and keep Gloria out of the way.
Dick Right.

Dick exits to Bedroom 1

Act I

Mike opens the door

Humbert Carpington enters. He is forty-five and eccentric

Mike Oh, good evening, Mr Carpington. Can I help you at all?

Mr Carpington Yes, Mr Feather you can. I have come here to complain and to complain loudly about excessive noise. I'm a patient man but there seems to be an extraordinary amount of comings and goings, doors opening and doors shutting, raised voices, lowered voices, footsteps running, footsteps walking. In fact, Mr Feather I have come to inform you that under the terms of the lease no sub-letting is allowed. Mr Feather how many persons are in this flat at the present moment?

Mike (*after looking at each bedroom door and making calculations on his fingers*) Just me and me mum, would you believe.

Mr Carpington No, I would not believe, and any more of it and I shall report you to the Management Committee for breaking Clauses three and six-a.

Mike Three and six-a. That's very bad.

Mr Carpington Indeed it is, Mr Feather. And furthermore, you're upsetting my little Bertie.

Mike I am sorry, Mr C. I didn't know you had any children.

Mr Carpington Mr Feather I am unmarried. Bertie is my beetle who lives in a matchbox by my bed.

Mike I am very sorry I have upset your little Bertie.

Mr Carpington He is not little, in fact, he's very large. He's been running round his matchbox all evening. He only does that when he's very upset.

Mike Do apologize to him for me. Would you like a drink?

Mr Carpington Certainly not. I never touch alcohol. Neither does Bertie. Although I did give him a drop of medicinal brandy when he was under the weather last summer.

Mike Did it make him better?

Mr Carpington Eventually, although he didn't stop running round his matchbox for a week. I thought he'd wear his little legs right out. Well, I must be getting back to make sure he's all right.

Mike I promise there won't be any more noise tonight.

Mr Carpington There had better not be, Mr Feather. I just hope that when I return to my flat Bertie and I will be able to sleep.

Mr Carpington exits through the front door. Marion enters from Bedroom 3

Marion Have you phoned Dick yet?

Mike No I haven't had the time. And now there's a further complication. Mother's arrived.

Marion Oh no! Where is she?

Mike In there.

Marion She mustn't see me with you. Look, you'd better get Dick over here as soon as possible so that I can leave quickly.

Mike Wouldn't it be better for you to leave now and we'll try again tomorrow?

Marion No, I've made up my mind, and I want you to phone Dick.
Mike What am I supposed to say to him? "Hallo, Dick, you must come immediately because I'm about to show Marion my continental quilt"?
Marion No, of course not. Don't be so silly. You'll have to pretend to be a well-wisher and say you know his wife's having an affair with his brother.
Mike Some well-wisher! What if he's not interested?
Marion Of course he'll be interested.
Mike Oh, very well. Go back to bed and I'll phone in a minute.
Marion What's wrong with phoning now?
Mike I don't feel up to it. My head.
Marion I'm sorry I'd forgotten. I'll go and get those pills.

Marion exits to Bedroom 3

Mike goes and has another drink. The doorbell rings. Mike goes and opens the front door

Julia Jones enters. She is twenty-two, beautiful—and dim

Julia Surprise, surprise.
Mike Julia—what are you doing back?
Julia Oh, Mike, I've come because I'm sorry we had that terrible quarrel. I've been so miserable that I decided I must come and tell you how very sorry I am.
Mike Not as sorry as I am.
Julia Darling, I knew you still loved me.
Mike Yes I do, but please go home. Please, please, please.
Julia (*starting to cry*) How can you say that if you love me? How can I go home? I've nowhere to go. I thought you'd be pleased to see me back so I gave up my flat and now you don't want me and I don't know what I'm going to do.
Mike Julia, it's not like that. I really am pleased to see you, only I've got people staying and I don't know where I'm going to put you.
Julia Put me! I'll sleep where I always sleep.
Mike I wish you could, but darling you can't. Please trust me. I can't explain now. Could you sleep in the bath? No, I didn't think you could. Just sit there while I try to think this out.

Dick enters from Bedroom 1

Dick Mike, I've been trying to explain to Gloria ...
Julia Who's Gloria?
Dick Who's this?
Julia Who are you?
Mike Just a minute and I'll get you the *Who's Who*.
Dick Well, I'm very pleased to meet you, whoever you are.
Julia I'm Julia. I'm Mike's "friend". Who are you?
Dick What, another "friend"?
Mike Yes, this is Julia. She's come back.
Dick Where from?

Act I

Mike I don't know. This is Dick, my brother.
Julia And who's Gloria?
Mike Gloria is er—er—er—Mr Carpington's girl friend. He lives next door.
Dick Is she?
Mike Yes, she is.
Dick Well, now we're all sorted out. Where are you going to sleep?
Mike She's not. She's going home.
Julia No, I'm not. I'm staying here with you.
Mike Look, Julia, it's just not possible . . .

The doorbell rings

You answer it, Dick. I can't stand any more surprises tonight.

Dick opens the door

Angela Leyton enters. She is twenty-two, beautiful and very sexy

Dick Angela!
Angela Oh Dick. I'm so glad to see you here. I didn't expect to be so lucky. I've been wandering about not knowing what to do, and then I suddenly thought of your brother and came here.
Mike Why me? Why couldn't you have thought of the butcher or the baker or the . . .
Angela Don't be silly, darling. I couldn't stay with them could I?
Mike Stay! Stay! You can't stay here either.
Angela But I can't go home while I'm so unhappy. Your wife was horrible to me, Dick. She didn't believe the story about the continental quilt.
Dick No, I know she didn't. What do you think I'm doing here?
Angela Who's that?
Mike This is Julia . . .
Julia This is Michael . . .
Dick This is Angela . . .
Angela This is Dick . . .
Mike Anyone else? No, no that's all.
Julia What were you saying about the continental quilt? Do tell me.
Dick Don't tell her.
Angela Well, Dick asked me round for a drink tonight and we got talking about bedding . . .
Julia Down?
Angela No, continental quilts. So he took me upstairs to see their new one.
Julia What was it like?
Angela Very warm.
Julia Well that's not much of a story.
Angela Ah, but I haven't got to the best bit . . .
Dick I think you've gone quite far enough.
Angela That's not what you said earlier.
Mike To leave out the interesting part, Dick's wife came home unexpectedly, and here they are.
Julia Oh, aren't wives boring. I'm glad you're not married.
Mike So am I.

Dick Yes it's all right for you.
Mike Well, you chose to get married—no-one forced you.
Dick Oh yes they did.
Mike Who forced you?
Dick Her father.
Mike You never told me that before.
Dick She'd only taken me upstairs to see her new bedspread, and he came back.
Mike Won't you ever learn? It's history repeating itself.
Dick Yes, but it's worse this time—there doesn't seem to be a way out.
Mike Trust me. I'll think of something. Let's all have a drink.
Julia Good idea.

Mike pours out drinks

Angela How did you meet Mike?
Julia That was rather funny as well. We met at a party. I went with someone else, and so did Mike. It turned out that I was with the husband and Mike was with the wife. They were both furious and went off to have a terrible row and we were left to console each other.
Angela Which you managed to do quite adequately.
Julia Oh yes, until we had the quarrel and I left and went and got a flat on my own.
Angela What did you quarrel about?
Julia I couldn't tell you that. You'd think it was silly.
Angela Go on, tell me.
Julia You won't laugh?
Angela I'll try not to.
Julia It was about . . . Oh no I can't tell you.
Angela Now I'm really intrigued. Whisper it to me, then.

Julia whispers in Angela's ear

   Whose turn it was?
Julia Yes.
Dick Whose turn it was to do what?
Julia Whose turn it was to put it on.
Mike That's not fair. It wasn't just that.
Julia No, I always squeezed too hard and made it bend in the middle.
Dick Put what on?
Angela Squeezed what too hard?
Mike The toothpaste tube, what else?
Julia Anyway, we won't quarrel about that again. I've brought my own this time.
Mike I still don't know where we're all going to sleep.

Gloria enters from Bedroom 1

Gloria What's going on out here? Who are they?
Dick Well, you know me.
Mike And you know me.

Act I

Gloria But I don't know them.
Mike No, you don't know them.
Dick No, she doesn't know them.
Gloria But I'd like to know them.
Mike But she'd like to know them. Dick, please introduce the ladies to Gloria.
Dick Do I know them? Oh yes of course I do. Gloria, this is Julia and Angela. Julia and Angela, this is Gloria.

Long pause

Gloria What are you doing here?
Julia }
Angela } We've come to stay. } *(Speaking together)*
Gloria Fine—have my room. I'm leaving.
Mike Now, Gloria, don't jump to conclusions. Angela is Dick's next-door neighbour. She's just come to see how he is.
Gloria How neighbourly.
Mike Yes, they're like that in Totteridge. Aren't you, Dick?
Dick Yes, we like it very much in Totteridge. I mean we're very much like it in Totteridge.
Gloria And Julia?
Mike Ah yes. Julia. Er—Julia is—er—Mr Carpington's real girl-friend. He lives next door but doesn't think it proper for his girl-friend to stay with him. (*He whispers to Julia*) I'll explain later.
Julia You'd just better.
Gloria Oh well, that's fine. I'll see what can be done about accommodating the ladies. Can three of us fit into a double bed? Well we'll just have to try. Come along, girls let's see what can be done. Have you got your night things with you?
Angela Of course. (*She produces a toothbrush*)

Gloria shepherds Julia and Angela into Bedroom 1

Julia But I want to . . .
Gloria Don't we all, dear. Come along.
Mike Four in a double bed. There's Dick as well.

Mike pushes Dick into Bedroom 1 after the girls

The doorbell rings. Mike opens the front door

Henry Feather, fifty-five, henpecked, enters

Dad, come in. Mum's in there.
Henry Well, in that case I'll sleep in there.

Before Mike can stop him, Henry goes into Bedroom 1, picking up a bottle of whisky as he passes the drinks table

Mike But Dad, Dad, you can't go . . . Oh, what the hell!

Marion enters from Bedroom 3

Marion I've found the pills. Take one of these and you'll soon feel better.
Mike Nothing can make me feel better.
Marion Don't be such an old misery. You've got to try and keep your mind on it or we won't get anywhere.
Mike Oh no, I've got to try and keep my mind off it or we will get somewhere.
Marion Now you run along and take these pills and then come back to me. I'll be waiting.
Mike Er—Marion, didn't we say we'd only pretend?
Marion I've had a much better idea. We'll pretend to pretend.
Mike Pretend to pretend. Oh, you mean that we should actually . . .
Marion Yes, darling, that's exactly what I mean.
Mike Oh no, it would put me in such an awkward position.
Marion Promises, promises.
Mike Er—Marion wait—I can't . . .
Marion Go and take those pills, then phone Dick up and then get in here.
Mike I—er—I er . . .
Marion Go on, hurry up—we haven't got all night. Oh, and take those pills with a little warm milk They'll work quicker that way.

Mike sighs heavily and exits to the kitchen, Marion exits to Bedroom 3. Mother enters from Bedroom 2 and knocks on Bedroom 3

Elizabeth Michael, Michael. Have you got a hot-water bottle? My feet are frozen. I'm missing Henry's back.

Gloria enters from Bedroom 1 and flits across to the bathroom

And where are you going?
Gloria To the bathroom. Do you mind?

Gloria exits to the bathroom

Elizabeth Impertinent hussy.

Mike enters from the kitchen

Mike I've put the milk on.
Elizabeth Milk! I want a hot-water bottle, not milk. Who have you put the milk on for?
Mike Um—Gloria. Gloria wants some warm milk.
Elizabeth Oh, that girl. She ought to be able to warm her own milk. Why should you do it for her?
Mike Because she's staying here and I must treat her like a guest.
Elizabeth That's always been your trouble Michael. You're much too kind to people. I think it's an imposition asking you to have her at all.
Mike I don't mind having her, Mother. She's no trouble.
Elizabeth Of course she's a trouble. She's asked you to warm milk for her.
Mike Well, it doesn't take long, and it is my kitchen. She wouldn't know where the saucepans were kept.
Elizabeth If she's got a tongue in her head—she can ask.
Mike Next time she wants anything—I'll tell her to get it herself.
Elizabeth I hope she'll be gone in the morning.

Act I

Mike I hope she won't.
Elizabeth Won't what?
Mike Won't want any more milk tonight. I've only got half a bottle left.
Elizabeth That is very bad organization. You knew that you would have an extra person staying therefore you should have ordered more milk.
Mike I didn't know I'd have two extra people staying, did I?
Elizabeth No, and I didn't know you'd have that girl staying, or I might have gone to Richard's instead.
Mike Oh, he's not there.
Elizabeth How do you know?
Mike I—er—I phoned earlier.
Elizabeth What for?
Mike To see if he was there.
Elizabeth Why?
Mike I just wanted a chat.
Elizabeth Oh, Michael, you were lonely—I'm so glad I came. I hate to think of you here alone at night.
Mike Mother, I am thirty-five.
Elizabeth No, dear, you can't be.
Mike I am, Mother.
Elizabeth Impossible.
Mike Mother, I've seen my birth certificate.
Elizabeth It must be a mistake. Since I'm only forty-five you can't possibly be more than twenty-five.
Mike Mother, I am thirty-five, quite capable of staying here alone at night, in fact very capable—and Mother, you are fifty-five.
Elizabeth Am I? I wonder how I became fifty-five. I was forty for years and then I added five so that makes me . . .
Mike Fifty-five.
Elizabeth You won't mention this to anyone, will you?
Mike Who would be interested?
Elizabeth Some members of my bridge club might be.
Mike I must remember that.

The doorbell rings. Mike opens the front door

Mr Carpington stands there

Mr Carpington—come in. Join us, please. The more the merrier.
Elizabeth Oh, Mr Carpington. Come in. I've already met your—(*sniff*)—lady-friend.
Mr Carpington You have. How very strange.
Elizabeth I'm bound to say I think it is strange. Are you sure you're doing the right thing? Marriage is a very serious step.
Mr Carpington Madam, I fail to see that my domestic arrangements are any of your business, but yours are very much mine. I will not, repeat not, put up with this disgraceful noise.
Elizabeth Noise, what noise? There's been no noise in this flat tonight. I know I've been here all the time.

Mr Carpington No noise. Are you deaf? There's been a continual stream of visitors, door bells ringing, footsteps, raised voices, lowered voices, women's voices, crying and a contravention of clause two-b.
Mike Or not two-b. I thought it was three and six-a.
Mr Carpington I cannot stand it any more. Sleep is beyond me. What can I do? What will you do about this dreadful noise?
Elizabeth (*to Mike*) Oh I see, mental is he? Don't worry I'll humour him. (*To Mr Carpington*) Mr Carpington I apologize for all the noise. It must have been most distressing for you, and I promise you we'll be very quiet from now on.
Mr Carpington I can see you are a lady, madam. It does make my mind feel a little less burdened.
Elizabeth Of course it does. Sit down, Mr Carpington. Let me get you some warm milk. I believe it should be made directly.
Mr Carpington Most kind, madam.
Elizabeth (*to Mike*) Quick, give me the brandy bottle. I'll lace it well—that'll make him sleep all right.
Mike But, Mother, I really think Mr Carpington should be getting home now. Shouldn't you Mr C.?
Mr Carpington No, young sir, some warm milk would be perfect.

Elizabeth exits to the kitchen. Gloria flits in with nighties in her arms, and exits to Bedroom 1

Did you see something?
Mike No, did you?
Mr Carpington It might have been a ghost.
Mike No couldn't have been—I'm not allowed ghosts under the terms of the lease.
Mr Carpington Perhaps I'm seeing things. It must be lack of sleep.

Marion's head comes round the door of Bedroom 3

Marion Have you phoned yet?
Mike Just going to.

Marion disappears again

Mr Carpington Did you hear a voice.
Mike Voice, Mr C.? What voice?
Mr Carpington I must be hearing things.

Julia's head comes round the door of Bedroom 1

Julia You've got a lot of explaining to do.
Mike Later, later.

Julia disappears again

Mr Carpington You must have heard that.
Mike What?
Mr Carpington I distinctly heard someone calling for a waiter.
Mike A waiter? What would anyone need a waiter for?

Act I

Elizabeth enters with a mug of milk

Mr C. has been hearing voices. Someone has been calling for a waiter.
Elizabeth (*giving the mug to Mr Carpington*) There, there, you drink this down and you'll feel better.
Mr Carpington That's very odd, this milk looks brown. (*He drinks*)
Mike It must have come from a dun cow.
Elizabeth Very well done, I would say.
Mr Carpington This warm milk is very soothing. (*Pause*) Madam, would you like to see my little Bertie.
Elizabeth I beg your pardon?
Mr Carpington My little Bertie. I have him here in my pocket.
Elizabeth Mr Carpington, I am not interested in what you have in your pocket.
Mike Go on, Mr C. Show her your Bertie.
Elizabeth Michael!
Mike It's black you know.
Elizabeth What is?
Mike His little Bertie.
Elizabeth Michael, don't encourage the man.
Mr Carpington I keep him in a matchbox.
Elizabeth In a matchbox?
Mr Carpington Oh yes. If I let him out he gets right out of hand. Once I showed him to a lady and she screamed and said it was the largest one she'd ever seen.
Elizabeth Drink up your warm milk, Mr Carpington. I think it's time we went to bed.
Mr Carpington Madam, I hardly know you . . .
Elizabeth I meant separately.
Mr Carpington Wouldn't you like even a quick peep?
Elizabeth No, thank you.
Mr Carpington I don't show him to everyone.
Elizabeth I'm most relieved to hear it. Just drink your milk and you'll soon be able to sleep.
Mr Carpington He's very shiny. I polish him every day.
Elizabeth Just what are you talking about?
Mr Carpington My Bertie. Here he is. (*He gets out a matchbox and opens it*)
Elizabeth Ugh, a beetle! He's horrible.
Mr Carpington Oh, now you've upset him. It's all right, Bertie. The lady didn't mean it. Look, madam, at the unusual markings on his back. (*He brings the matchbox very close to Elizabeth*)

Elizabeth tries to push the matchbox away. It overturns, and the beetle falls down the front of her nightdress

Elizabeth Oh no, help me! Get it out at once!
Mr Carpington If you'll allow me, madam. (*He goes to put his hand down the front of her nightdress*)
Elizabeth How dare you, you dreadful man! Michael, do something. Help me.

Mr Carpington May I suggest that you jiggle about a bit and then Bertie might fall out.

Elizabeth shakes herself and Bertie falls out

Ah here he is. (*Picking it up*) Poor little Bertie—what a ghastly experience for you. What a terrible fright you've had my poor little Bertie. I would ask you to be more careful in future, madam.
Elizabeth Bother your beetle! What about me? Having that dreadful thing down my nightgown. Thank heavens I wear a vest.
Mike Are you all right, Mother?
Elizabeth No, I'm not all right.
Mike Allow me to get you some warm milk to soothe you.
Elizabeth Make sure it comes from a dun cow then.
Mike Well done?
Elizabeth Very well done.

Mike exits to the kitchen

Mr Carpington Poor Bertie, are you better now? Yes, that's right—you go to sleep. You did like him really, didn't you.
Elizabeth He was very—er—very unusual.
Mr Carpington Oh yes, I think so too. He has quite a personality of his own.
Elizabeth I'm sure he has.
Mr Carpington What a lovely colour your dressing gown is, madam.
Elizabeth How kind of you to say so.
Mr Carpington It reminds me of Bertie's head with the sun on it.
Elizabeth Oh! Do you have any more pets?
Mr Carpington Oh yes, I have a tarantula called Tommy.
Elizabeth Not with you, surely?
Mr Carpington Oh no, I keep him in the bathroom. I've noticed he has a very strange effect on people.
Elizabeth You've nothing else with you?
Mr Carpington No, only Bertie. Do sit down and tell me about yourself.
Elizabeth Where shall I begin?

Mike enters from the kitchen with a mug of milk

Mike Not at the beginning or we'll be here all night. (*He gives it to Elizabeth*)
Elizabeth I was born on a small farm. . .
Mr Carpington I expect there were a lot of Berties there.
Mike Please, Mother, it's late , I'm tired. Let's get to bed.
Mr Carpington Young man, I find your attitude to your mother rude in the extreme. Pray continue, Mrs Feather. I want to hear all about the Berties on the farm.
Elizabeth Are you really interested in my farm?
Mr Carpington Yes, Mrs Feather, I really am.
Elizabeth Please call me Elizabeth.
Mr Carpington It would be a great pleasure, Elizabeth, and you must call me Humbert.

Act I

Elizabeth Oh, must I?
Mr Carpington Indeed you must, Elizabeth. Now do continue.
Elizabeth Where had I got to?
Mike Near the end I think.
Mr Carpington You were going to tell me about the Berties on the farm.
Mike Mother, please.

A hand comes round the door of Bedroom 1 and takes another bottle from the drinks table

Mr Carpington Did you see that?
Mike See what?
Mr Carpington A hand.
Mike What hand?

The hand comes round again and takes a glass

Mr Carpington That hand.
Mike Where?
Mr Carpington It's gone.
Elizabeth There, there Humbert, just relax.

During the following dialogue there are definite sounds of a party going on in Bedroom 1

Mr Carpington I'm sure I heard something then.
Elizabeth Let me get you some more warm milk.
Mr Carpington Thank you, Elizabeth. That would be very civil of you.

Elizabeth exits to the kitchen

Wonderful woman your mother.
Mike Don't you feel at all tired? It's time you went home.
Mr Carpington Really, young man, your manners are appalling.

Henry's head appears round the door of Bedroom 1

Henry Mike, which one's mine?
Mike Take your pick.
Mr Carpington How dare you, young sir!
Mike How dare I what?
Mr Carpington Call me a dry old stick.
Mike I didn't. I said—er—I am Mick.
Mr Carpington Yes, I know you are, although I do not approve of shortening names.
Mike What about Bertie then?
Mr Carpington He doesn't approve either.

Elizabeth enters from the kitchen with the milk

Mike Here's your milk. Drink it up and go.
Elizabeth Michael, is there something bothering you? Don't you feel yourself tonight?
Mike Oh I won't, Mother, I promise you.

Elizabeth You won't promise me what?
Mike Whatever it is we're talking about.
Elizabeth I'm getting confused. Michael, are you well?
Mike I expect I am but I haven't time to think about it. No, no I'm not. I must go to bed at once. Come along, Mr C., time for you to go home so I can get to bed.

A crash is heard from Bedroom 1

Elizabeth What was that?
Mike What?
Elizabeth I thought I heard something.
Mike Not you as well.
Mr Carpington I'm sure I did but I really don't care any more.
Elizabeth There, that was a definite chinking of glasses. Michael, just what is going on in your third bedroom?
Mike I dread to think.
Elizabeth I beg your pardon?
Mike It must be the sink. It often gurgles and clinks.

A laugh is heard

Elizabeth But, Michael, does it also laugh?
Mike Oh yes, all the time. It has a wonderful sense of humour.
Elizabeth I insist you open that door at once.
Mike Oh well. (*He goes to the door, muttering*) What the...
Elizabeth What did you say?
Mike The door's stuck.
Elizabeth Try pulling it, Michael.
Mike No good, still stuck.
Elizabeth Harder, Michael.
Mike (*opening the door*) Come on out, all of you. Come and face the music. The game's up.

Henry, Dick, Julia, Angela, and Gloria enter from Bedroom 1, giggling and laughing

Henry Elizabeth, what are you doing with that man?
Elizabeth Henry, what are you doing with that woman?
Mike What have you been doing with the girls?

Marion enters from Bedroom 3

Dick What have you been doing in Mike's bedroom?
Marion What are you doing with her? Been looking at continental quilts again?
Julia \
Gloria / Who's that? { (*Speaking together*)
Mike This is Mr Carpington from next door.
Julia \
Gloria / Oh my boy-friend. { (*Speaking together*)

They go and sit one on either knee of Mr Carpington

Elizabeth Two girl-friends. Really, Humbert, you should be more careful at your age. As for you two, I can only offer you a word of advice. Always wear a vest when you are anywhere near him.

The doorbell rings

Mike Now who could this be? I don't think I have any more relatives to come unless of course it's a long lost cousin from Outer Mongolia. Come in whoever you are. (*He opens the door*)

Miss Priscilla Plankton enters

Miss Plankton Oh, is it a pyjama party, or can anyone join in?
Mike Yes, come in, bring the whole street, the whole town, the whole country . . .
Miss Plankton Oh Mr Feather, I've come alone. Should I have brought a partner?
Mike No Miss Plankton, you should not. But let me explain—this is not a party.
Miss Plankton Not?
Mike Not.
Miss Plankton Oh well, I won't stay then.
Mike You won't stay? Then you're the first one tonight. Did you come for anything special.
Miss Plankton Well, yes, I did, as a matter of fact.
Mike Is it something I can help you with?
Miss Plankton Yes, I did come to see you.
Mike Well?
Miss Plankton It's rather personal. I was hoping to see you alone.
Mike Alone. Well you've picked the wrong flat and the wrong time. I've never been less alone in my life.
Miss Plankton I can see you're rather crowded. I thought it was a party. I so love parties.
Mike No this is merely a gathering of my nearest and dearest. I hope to go to bed soon. In fact, I've been hoping for the last hour.
Miss Plankton Am I keeping you up?
Mike You and eight others.
Miss Plankton I'll come back another time. I really must see you alone.
Mike This matter that I can help you with—it has to be you and I alone?
Miss Plankton Oh, most definitely.
Mike Couldn't you give me a little hint?
Miss Plankton It's something that you don't need any hints about.
Mike Oh no. I've got enough trouble without that.
Miss Plankton Without what?
Mike Whatever it is I've got to see you about.
Miss Plankton Oh yes, that.
Mike What?
Miss Plankton That about which I must see you alone.
Mike I think we're going round in circles here. Now have I got this straight.

You want to see me alone, you can't tell me what it is about because of all my visitors. Right?
Miss Plankton Right.
Mike Well, in that case I suggest you come back in the morning. With a bit of luck I might be less crowded by then.
Miss Plankton Yes, Michael, I'll go now. You're quite sure it isn't a party?
Mike Quite, quite sure.
Miss Plankton I am sorry, because I love parties, but no-one invites me very often. I once went to one but was so shy I hid behind the potted plant, and I just sat there on my own until a gentleman came and asked if I was . . .
Elizabeth Half-witted, I should think,.
Mike Mother!
Elizabeth This is the female, Michael. The mad one I was telling you about.
Mike Oh no, Mother, this is Miss Plankton. She lives the other side.
Miss Plankton Yes, I've lived next to Michael for a long time now.
Mike Well, now you're here I'd better introduce you so that there are no further misunderstandings. This is Miss Plankton everyone. This is my mother, father, brother, sister-in-law . . .
Elizabeth All right, all right, Michael. That's quite enough. Miss Plankton isn't interested in our family or its affairs.
Miss Plankton Affairs?
Elizabeth Yes that is the right word to use tonight, Henry, just what have you been up to?
Henry Well, dear, I thought . . .
Elizabeth That is your trouble—you will keep thinking. I've told you before you should leave it all to me.
Henry Yes, dear.
Elizabeth I'm still waiting for an explanation.
Henry I was trying to tell you when you interrupted . . .
Elizabeth I don't want any excuses. I want an explanation.
Henry Yes, dear.
Mike Mother. I think it would be better if we sorted this out later.
Elizabeth If we leave it any later it will be morning.
Mike Yes, Mother, you're absolutely right. We must all get to bed.
Elizabeth That is not what I meant.
Henry Well, dear, I am very tired.
Elizabeth Are you, Henry? Just what have you been doing to make you so tired?
Dick Mother, I think it would be better if we didn't quarrel in front of Miss Plankton.
Miss Plankton I don't mind at all.
Elizabeth Richard, your opinion has not been asked for. I must get to the very bottom of all this.
Dick Oh, must you?
Elizabeth Yes, I must. Marion, now, let's start with you. What are you doing here?
Marion I er—I don't know. What am I doing here, Mike?

Act I 27

Mike How should I know. Ask Dick.
Dick Don't ask me. I didn't know you were here did I? Ask Dad.
Henry I don't know. I've only been in there. I didn't know you were here.
Elizabeth Does anyone know why Marion is here?
Mike No, I didn't know, did I? Did I? No, I'm sure I didn't. Did you know you were here, Marion?
Elizabeth Of course she knew she was here. It's why she is here that seems to be a complete mystery.
Miss Plankton Oh, I like a mystery. Have you read *The Seven Dials Murder*?
Elizabeth *The Seven Dials Murder*. Isn't that by Agatha Christie? Yes, I believe I have. Not as good as some of her others.
Miss Plankton Indeed no. Our local library has them all. I had to wait three weeks to get *Curtain*, though.
Elizabeth Oh yes, I've read that. I found it very disappointing.
Miss Plankton I didn't guess who the murderer was though, did you?
Elizabeth No, I didn't. Miss Plankton will you please stop side-tracking me. It's the mystery in this room that interests me at the moment. Now then—(*pointing to Julia*)—you say you are Mr Carpington's girl-friend—but where did you come from and how did you know he was here? Did you tell her to come here, Humbert?
Mr Carpington (*trying to disguise his voice*) No, I've never seen her before.
Julia Yes you have—I am your girl-friend.
Gloria No, you're not. I am.
Elizabeth Mr Carpington, I think you've got some explaining to do.
Miss Plankton Not Humbert Carpington?

Mr Carpington pulls Julia and Gloria in front of his face. Miss Plankton parts them.

Oh, Humbert—how could you?
Elizabeth What is this man to you?
Miss Plankton He's my boy-friend.
Elizabeth Oh, you monster!
Julia Deceiver!
Gloria Three-timer!
Miss Plankton Bluebeard!

The ladies start hitting Humbert with cushions

Mr Carpington Ladies please stop—oh you've squashed my little Bertie.

CURTAIN

ACT II

The same. The following morning

Dick is discovered, drinking a cup of coffee. Mike enters from the front door, carrying two bottles of milk. He ignores Dick, goes to the kitchen, returns with a cup of coffee and sits as far away from Dick as possible. They look at each other three times, then away again

Mike I suppose you think it's all my fault.
Dick Of course it is you—you—wife-snatcher.
Mike That's better.
Dick What do you mean—that's better?
Mike Last night you called me an old lecher. I bitterly resent the old.
Dick Well, you are a lecher. What were you doing with Marion in your bedroom?
Mike Well, I wasn't showing her my continental quilt.
Dick No doubt you have the perfect explanation.
Mike Dick, would I lie to you?
Dick Yes, if you thought I'd believe you.
Mike Dick, this is the truth. Marion came here last night and wanted us to pretend to have an affair.
Dick What you and I?
Mike No, you idiot—Marion and I!
Dick But why?
Mike Well, in her illogical womanly way, she thought you wouldn't like it.
Dick She was wrong.
Mike You mean you do like it?
Dick No, I mean I very much don't like it. In fact, Mike, I could strangle you.
Mike Me! I'm sure if violence is needed it ought to be used on Marion. She suggested it, not me.
Dick You didn't need to go along with it. Why didn't you tell me she was here?
Mike Because I thought you might try and strangle me, and I was right. Look, Dick, Marion only wanted to make you jealous.
Dick And you only wanted to make Marion.
Mike I say, that was rather good.
Dick Yes, it was, wasn't it. Oh, I'm sorry Mike—only I don't know what I'm going to do. She doesn't believe that I was only in that bedroom trying to keep out of Mother's way.
Mike How very surprising!
Dick Yes, it is. What can I do now?

Act II

Mike I thought I told you before, you must learn from me. Now I'm in a lot of trouble too but am I despairing— no, I'm not. Am I panicking— no I'm not. Am I cool, calm and collected—of course I am.
Dick What shall we do if Mother comes in?
Mike Run like hell—what else?
Dick Where is Mother?
Mike Let's see. I think the three girls are in there—(*Indicating Bedroom 1*) —I don't dare go in because if they've been talking—I'm finished. Mother is in there—(*Indicating Bedroom 2*)—and Dad and Mr C. are in my room. I slept on the sofa. Where did you sleep?
Dick In the bath. Did you know the cold tap drips?
Mike That must have cooled your ardour.
Dick Cooled my what?
Mike Your ardour.
Dick Oh no, it was dripping on my feet. What happened to that funny lady-friend of Mr C.'s? The real one, I mean.
Mike I don't know. I expect she's in her flat. She gave him an earful and ran out crying. Where's Marion, by the way?
Dick I don't know. She gave me an earful and ran out crying. I expect she's at home packing her bags by now.
Mike I don't suppose you'd like to join her?
Dick Not until I've had something to fortify me.
Mike It's a bit early to start drinking.
Dick I meant a few aspirins, to get rid of this hangover.
Mike Come on, then. I've got some in the kitchen and then we've got some quick thinking to do.

Mike and Dick exit to the kitchen. Elizabeth enters from Bedroom 2 and exits to the bathroom. Henry enters from Bedroom 3 and exits to the kitchen. Julia and Gloria enter from Bedroom 1

Gloria What a night! Three in a double bed just doesn't work.
Julia Not when the other two are girls.
Gloria Are you really Humbert's girl-friend? What can you possibly see in him?
Julia Absolutely nothing. I thought you were his girl-friend, not me. I was only pretending.
Gloria So was I.
Julia What are you doing here, then?
Gloria I might ask you the same question. I live here.
Julia So do I.
Gloria Well, you weren't here when I moved in yesterday.
Julia No, I left two weeks ago, but now I've come back.
Gloria I see. I'm sorry, but your vacancy has been filled.
Julia So I see. No wonder Mike wasn't very pleased to see me last night.
Gloria He must have been horrified. As though he didn't have enough problems, then his old cast-off turns up.
Julia Old cast-off! What a cheek! Well, this old cast-off is going to be cast on again.

Gloria Sorry, love, there's not room for both of us.
Julia Oh, well, you'll just have to go again, then.
Gloria No chance. I like it here. I've never seen so much action in one small flat before.
Julia Look, I can't go because I've given up my flat and I'll be homeless.
Gloria If I may say so, you should have thought about that before.
Julia I know, but that's always been my trouble. I think very slowly.
Gloria What about Dick? Couldn't you transfer your affections to him?
Julia No, I don't think I could. He's married, and I don't fancy living with his wife as well.
Gloria That's not quite what I had in mind.
Julia Well, we could toss for him. Heads yours, tails mine.
Gloria No dear, I never do things by half. Perhaps it would be better if we asked him to make up his own mind.
Julia Oh no, that wouldn't do. I would feel so sorry for you when he chose me.
Gloria Are you so sure he would?
Julia Of course he would. He loves me.
Gloria He loves me as well.
Julia I think I have an idea.
Gloria This should be good.
Julia Let's both stay here and share him.
Gloria It's an idea, but would it work? Would we get on together?
Julia Oh no, only one at a time. We could take turns.
Gloria What about housework and things like that?
Julia We'll work out a rota.
Gloria But what if he doesn't agree?
Julia We'll rewrite the rota.
Gloria I mean, with us both staying.
Julia Two against one. He hasn't really got much choice.
Gloria No you're right. There's not a lot he can do.
Julia I hope there is.
Gloria Come on, then, let's get something worked out. Night shifts first.

Julia and Gloria exit to Bedroom 1, still talking. Father enters from the kitchen with a cup of coffee, as Elizabeth enters from the bathroom

Henry sees her and tries to sneak back to the kitchen

Elizabeth Henry, I want a word with you.
Henry I thought you might.
Elizabeth Yes, I'm waiting to hear your explanation of your eccentric behaviour last night. Just what were you doing in that bedroom?
Henry Well dear, I didn't know there was anyone there when I arrived and I just went straight in and there they were—all six of them.
Elizabeth But there were only three.
Henry I must have been seeing double.
Elizabeth And what was Dick doing in there?
Henry Hiding.
Elizabeth Hiding from whom?

Act II

Henry You.
Elizabeth Why was he hiding from me?
Henry He didn't want you to know he'd left Marion.
Elizabeth I'm ashamed of you both behaving in such a disgraceful manner. Were you drinking as well?
Henry As well as what?
Elizabeth As well as Richard?
Henry Oh no, he's rather better at it than I am.
Elizabeth Henry! Something's got to be done about Richard. I want you to cut off his allowance. I am seriously worried about the influence he's having on Michael. Michael lives an exemplary life and I am afraid that Richard is setting him a very bad example. If you deprive him of his allowance he might see the error of his ways and reform.
Henry Poor old Dick. Are you sure that Mike is so blameless?
Elizabeth Of course he is. He takes after me. I was here last night and saw what went on. Richard was to blame for everything.
Henry But who were those lovely girls, then?
Elizabeth That dreadful Mr Carpington's girl-friends. Can you imagine having three girl-friends?
Henry No—more's the pity!
Elizabeth Henry! I think the man's quite mad.
Henry Yes—didn't he take a fancy to you?
Elizabeth Henry!
Henry Sorry, dear.
Elizabeth If you think I would look at a man who carried a beetle around in a matchbox you are very much mistaken. In fact, Henry, it has made me see you in a new light.
Henry Me?
Elizabeth Yes, Henry, you have your faults, a great many of them, I have to say—but I am glad that in all the years I've known you, you have never carried anything revolting around in your pocket.
Henry Thank you, dear.
Elizabeth Yes, Henry, I have decided to forgive you for your disgraceful behaviour and I shall return home with you later.
Henry Thank you, dear.
Elizabeth But the television set must go.
Henry Oh no.
Elizabeth Henry!
Henry Yes, dear?
Elizabeth Now that we have solved all your problems—what are we going to do about Richard and Marion? (*Pause*) Well, Henry?
Henry I'm waiting for you tell me, dear.
Elizabeth I shall talk to Marion, woman to woman, and you will talk to Richard, man to man. Can you manage that, Henry?
Henry Talk to Richard, man to man.
Elizabeth Sort him out, tell him what's what, man to man.
Henry Man to man.
Elizabeth That's the idea.

Henry Sort him out, tell him what's what, man to man. Good, fine, that's settled. (*Pause*) What have I got to say?
Elizabeth Come in here Henry and I shall tell you exactly what to say.

Elizabeth and Henry exit to Bedroom 2. Angela enters from Bedroom 1 and sits forlornly on the sofa. Mr Carpington enters from Bedroom 3

Angela Good morning. Did you sleep well?
Mr Carpington No, I didn't. I'm so upset. What am I to do? Miss Plankton will never believe me when I tell her that I'm quite innocent of the slanderous charges that she made against me.
Angela Where is she this morning?
Mr Carpington In her flat, I expect.
Angela You don't look well.
Mr Carpington Of course I'm not well. That milk had a very strange effect on me last night. It made my head ache and my heart ache.
Angela What a shame!
Mr Carpington And I've buried my little Bertie this morning.
Angela You have?
Mr Carpington Yes, I've put him in the window box between the begonias.
Angela You mustn't be sad. You'll find another beetle.
Mr Carpington Not like my Bertie.
Angela Well, perhaps not.
Mr Carpington What am I to do? I've lost my beloved and my pet.
Angela I'm sure I could try and explain to Miss Plankton for you.
Mr Carpington What could you possibly say?
Angela I don't know. Could I say you had temporary amnesia, and that you'd forgotten about the two nieces you had on your kneesies.
Mr Carpington No, that's no good. I've got no family.
Angela What about saying you were protecting two innocent girls in a den of vice.
Mr Carpington She'll want to know what I was doing in a den of vice.
Angela Well, what were you doing?
Mr Carpington I came in to complain about the noise.
Angela Oh, was there some noise then?
Mr Carpington Of course there was. A party was in progress in one bedroom and what was going on in the others, I shudder to think.
Angela Humbert, have you by any chance, proposed to Miss Plankton.
Mr Carpington No I haven't. I've wanted to for a long time but I can never find the words.
Angela Mr C., your troubles are over.
Mr Carpington What do you mean?
Angela That's your answer.
Mr Carpington What is?
Angela Propose to her and I'll guarantee she'll forget the rest.
Mr Carpington You mean, ask her to marry me?
Angela Of course. What did you think I meant?
Mr Carpington My dear young lady I would be most honoured if Miss

Act II   33

Plankton would accept my hand in marriage but I really don't think I could ask her.
Angela Why ever not?
Mr Carpington I can't find the words. Whenever I start to propose I find myself asking something quite different.
Angela Really!
Mr Carpington Why yes. Last time I started "my dear Priscilla would you do me the honour of . . ."
Angela Yes?
Mr Carpington Then I dried up and muttered " the honour of looking at my new washing machine . . ."
Angela Safer than continental quilts.
Mr Carpington Indeed, but it didn't get me to the point I wanted to be at.
Angela No, I can imagine. You must let me help you.
Mr Carpington Oh, could you?
Angela Yes, I'm sure I could.
Mr Carpington I'm a very slow learner. Could I take notes?
Angela Yes if it would help but try not to refer to them while proposing.
Mr Carpington That wouldn't help?
Angela No, that wouldn't help.
Mr Carpington What do I have to say then? (*He gets out a notebook and pencil*)
Angela You must look into her eyes and say—what's her name?
Mr Carpington (*writing*) I must look into her eyes and say "What's her name?"
Angela No—what's her name?
Mr Carpington Yes, I've got that down.
Angela No, your lady-friend—what's her name?
Mr Carpington Oh, I see. Her name is Priscilla.
Angela Right, you say "Priscilla, what beautiful blue/grey/green eyes you have."
Mr Carpington (*writing*) Priscilla, what beautiful blue/grey/green eyes you have.
Angela No, only one of them.
Mr Carpington (*writing*) Priscilla, what a beautiful blue/grey/green eye you have.
Angela No, no, no. Only one colour.
Mr Carpington Which one?
Angela The colour her eyes are.
Mr Carpington But I don't know the colour her eyes are.
Angela No—but you will when you've looked into them.
Mr Carpington Right, I've got that. Look into eyes and ascertain the colour.
Angela Good. "What lovely hair you have."
Mr Carpington Oh, thank you very much.
Angela No, not you, Priscilla.
Mr Carpington Has she?
Angela I don't know but you must say it.

Mr Carpington (*writing*) Must say it.
Angela Then you say "In fact you are altogether beautiful."
Mr Carpington Don't go too fast. I've got to write it down.
Angela Then take her hand and say "What pretty hands you've got, I'd like to kiss them."
Mr Carpington And do I?
Angela Of course you do.
Mr Carpington (*writing*) Of course I do.
Angela Then, "My darling Priscilla I can't think about anything but you. You're constantly on my mind. Please, Priscilla, will you marry me?"
Mr Carpington And then what?
Angela Hopefully she will say "Yes", and you will take her in your arms and kiss her.
Mr Carpington I don't know if I can manage that.
Angela Have I to teach you everything?
Mr Carpington Oh yes. Everything.
Angela Where can we go? I know let's try Mike's room. Come on, I'll give you some free tuition.
Mr Carpington If you're sure you know what you're doing.
Angela Yes and how to do it.

Angela and Mr Carpington exit into Bedroom 3. Mike and Dick enter from the kitchen

Mike It will work. I know women.
Dick I'm not so sure.
Mike All you have to do is to lie groaning a bit, and she'll feel so sorry for you she'll take you home and comfort you.
Dick I just hope you're right. I could do with some comfort.
Mike I would have thought you'd had plenty last night.
Dick Speak for yourself—I slept in the bath, remember?
Mike I do remember, but what about earlier? You were in that bedroom for quite some time with Angela, weren't you?
Dick There were five of us in there, and there's scarcely room to swing a cat.
Mike What's that got to do with it?
Dick I'm just pointing out that there were five of us crammed into one small bedroom, plus two bottles of Scotch, and it was none too comfortable.
Mike Oh, I'm so sorry. Next time you find yourself in such a position—please feel free to use my bedroom.
Dick All right, I will, but with any luck and sufficient acting skills perhaps I'll be able to use my own.
Mike That's the spirit, but remember that if Plan A fails you must immediately switch to Plan B.
Dick Plan B?
Mike Yes, bribery.
Dick Oh, what shall I bribe her with?
Mike Whatever she wants most.

Act II

Dick What's that?
Mike How should I know? She's your wife, not mine.
Dick Well, she did mention she needed a new toaster.
Mike A new toaster. Are you insane? It will have to be a much bigger bribe than that.
Dick I shall have to think about it.
Mike If you do that you're finished.
Dick What do you mean?
Mike You won't have time to think about it. If Plan A fails you'll immediately have to snap into action with Plan B. "Darling I'm sorry but I'll make it up to you. Please forgive me and remember that I'll always love you and you alone. Please let me show you how much I care. Would you like a trip around the world or a fabulous diamond ring or an electric toaster?"
Dick Oh, I see what you mean. But if it doesn't work I shall hold you responsible.
Mike Trust big brother.
Dick I'll try.
Mike Now then, what about me? What am I going to do about Gloria and Julia?
Dick I don't know but if you need any assistance . . .
Mike You keep out of this. You mustn't get involved any more. But I'm going to have to ask one of them to go, and I don't know which one. You see, I have troubles, too.
Dick Oh, to have such troubles! Don't you like one more than the other?
Mike No, they're both lovely.
Dick Why don't you toss for it then? Heads Julia. Tails Gloria.
Mike No, that wouldn't be fair on the one that lost. Perhaps I should let them choose. Make their own decision.
Dick Don't do that they might fight over you. You wouldn't want to cause bloodshed.
Mike No, you're right. I must be the one to decide.
Dick Last in—first out they say.
Mike Yes, but the last in was the first in that went away and came back to be the last in, and the second in was last in because she came after the last in who was really the first in, but the second in was here when the first in returned. So which should it be?
Dick Could you repeat that?
Mike No, I don't think I could.
Dick Let's worry about you later. It's far more important to make Marion take me back before Mother makes Dad cut off my allowance.
Mike I don't think he would, not after the way he behaved last night.
Dick Twenty-four hours with Mother and he'll do as he's told.
Mike (*going to the telephone*) Right. I'll phone Marion. Get ready to groan in the background. (*He dials a number*)
Dick (*lying on the sofa*) Groan, groan.
Mike Louder, louder.
Dick *Groan, groan.*

Mike Keep it up. That's fine. (*On the telephone*) Oh hallo, Marion. Guess who?... Oh, there's no need to be like that.... I'm afraid I've got some very bad news for you.... No, no he hasn't shot himself.... No, he's fallen down the stairs.... No stairs in a flat?... Ah, yes, you're right, just testing your reflexes this morning.... He tripped over the sofa.... Of course he hadn't been drinking. He's very badly hurt and is asking for you.... Yes, I'm sure it's you.... You will?... Oh, that's wonderful. He will be pleased. See you soon. Good bye. (*To Dick*) She's coming but she doesn't sound very convinced.

Elizabeth enters from Bedroom 2. Mike exits to the kitchen very quickly Dick tries to follow

Elizabeth Richard, I want a word with you.
Dick Can't it wait? I'm busy.
Elizabeth Busy—lying on the sofa?
Dick Oh, how did you know I was lying?
Elizabeth Richard, I want to know exactly what has been going on between you and that woman.
Dick Which woman?
Elizabeth Marion.
Dick Oh, her?
Elizabeth Yes, her. I mean Marion.
Dick My wife?
Elizabeth Yes, your wife. Only no-one would believe it. You spend all your time staying with Michael and myself.
Dick Oh no, that's simply not true. I distinctly remember spending three days with Marion this week, and, why, it must have been four days the week before...
Elizabeth Richard, it is not good enough. Unless you can make some permanent arrangement to stay at home I shall have to take drastic measures to see that you do.
Dick A straight-jacket, did you have in mind, or manacles, perhaps?
Elizabeth No Richard, no manacles and no allowance.
Dick Yes, Mother.
Elizabeth Your father also wants a word with you. (*She opens the door of Bedroom 3*) Henry, come here and talk to Richard.

Henry enters

Henry Hallo, Dick.
Dick Hallo, Dad.
Elizabeth Henry, say what I've told you to say.
Henry Yes, dear. Er—Dick—um—er—I think it's time we had a little chat.
Elizabeth Henry—get on with it.
Henry Yes, dear. Well, Dick, your mother and I—well it's more your mother really...
Elizabeth Henry!
Henry Yes, dear. As I was saying, your mother and I feel it's time that you took life a little more seriously and tried to settle down a bit.

Act II

Dick O.K., Dad, I know what you're going to say, so you can save yourself the trouble.
Elizabeth (*prodding him*) How dare you speak to your father in such a manner. Now listen to me, Richard, if we have any more nonsense from you we'll disown you. Do you understand? You'll never receive another penny from us. Is that clear. (*She advances towards Dick, prodding him until he falls over the back of the sofa*)
Dick Oh my back, my back! I think it's broken.
Elizabeth Richard, Richard are you all right. (*She helps him onto the sofa*)
Dick Oh, it's my back. I think I'm permanently damaged. (*Groan, groan*)

Mike enters from the kitchen

Mike Oh, very realistic, Dick. I like it.
Elizabeth Your brother has hurt his back—call a doctor immediately.
Mike Oh, don't be fooled by that. He's just pretending.
Elizabeth Don't be so callous. Call a doctor.
Mike No, I won't It's only a game.
Elizabeth Michael, I never thought I would see such an unfeeling side to your nature. Your poor brother is lying here injured, and you say it's a game. Call the doctor at once.
Mike No, I won't.
Dick (*weakly*) Mike, Mike . . .

Mike goes to him

(*Whispering*) I did fall off, but I'm perfectly all right, but it's taken her mind off Marion. (*In his normal voice*) It's real. I did fall.
Mike Really real?
Dick Really real.
Elizabeth Of course it's real. Now we must get a doctor, but I don't know whether . . .
Dick I've just remembered. Angela's a doctor.
Elizabeth What a stroke of luck! Where is she?
Dick Somewhere around, although I haven't seen her this morning.
Mike Just hold on and I'll make a quick search. (*He opens Bedroom 1 and blows kisses to the girls. He opens Bedroom 2*) No, empty. (*He opens Bedroom 3*) Oh, sorry if I'm interrupting anything.

Angela and Mr Carpington enter from Bedroom 3

Angela We were just practising.
Mike Sorry to have interrupted. Some people have all the luck.
Angela Oh poor Dick, what's happened to you?
Dick I fell over the sofa and hurt my back.
Angela (*examining him*) Does that hurt?

Dick groans

And that?

Dick groans more loudly

And that?

Dick gives a very loud groan

I don't think it's too bad. Help me get him into the bedroom so that I can get him undressed and examine him properly.

Mr Carpington and Mike help Dick into Bedroom 3. Angela follows them

Elizabeth Henry, this is all your fault for being too hard on him.
Henry Yes, dear.
Elizabeth Another time try to be more careful, and remember we're all humans with human failings. No-one's perfect, not even my son.

Mike and Mr Carpington enter from Bedroom 3

And I don't think much of your behaviour, either.
Mike Mine!
Elizabeth Yes, yours. If you're not careful I shall get your father to cut you out of his will.
Mike Not again!
Elizabeth What did you say?
Mike What a shame.
Elizabeth Now then, Henry, come and help me to pack. We're leaving this den of iniquity.

Elizabeth and Henry exit to Bedroom 2

Mr Carpington Where can I go, I've got some studying to do?
Mike Kitchen's probably the quietest place.

Mr Carpington exits to the kitchen

The door bell rings. Mike opens the door

Marion enters

Oh hello, Marion. Nice day, isn't it.
Marion Let me in at once. Where's Dick?
Mike Dick, Dick who?
Marion My husband, your brother.
Mike Oh, that Dick.
Marion Well?
Mike No, he's not actually. The doctor's with him now.
Marion Where?
Mike In there, but you mustn't go in. The doctor said no-one was to go in whilst he was being examined.
Marion I'll wait here, then. What seems to be the matter with him?
Mike Back trouble. He fell over the sofa, you know.
Marion Yes, I did know—you told me on the phone.
Mike Did I? I must be physic. It hadn't happened then.
Marion What hadn't happened?
Mike Well, it had happened, only not properly.
Marion What hadn't happened properly?
Mike The back trouble. It got worse later. He's been in agony with it.
Marion Oh, poor Dick.

Act II

Mike Nearly crying with the pain.
Marion Oh, and to think I didn't believe you when you phoned.
Mike Poor, poor Dick.
Marion Mike, do you think I misjudged him last night?
Mike Of course you did, Marion. It wasn't that he wanted to be in there drinking and entertaining Mr C.'s lady-friends. He only wanted to keep out of Mother's way and he couldn't help Angela following him here, could he?
Marion I've been very unfair to him. I'll have to make it up somehow. That doctor must have finished now. I'm going in.
Mike No, don't do that.
Marion Why not? He's my husband.
Mike The doctor said we mustn't.
Marion Well how long does it take, for goodness sake?
Mike Half-an-hour on average.
Marion What, to make an examination?
Mike Oh no, longer if you do that.
Marion What rubbish—I'm going in.
Mike No, don't. I've got something to show you.
Marion Can't it wait?
Mike No it can't. Come along. Quickly now.

Mike pushes Marion out to the kitchen. Mr Carpington enters from the kitchen

Mr Carpington I was trying to study. Where can I go now?
Mike Try the bathroom.

Mike exits to the kitchen, and Mr Carpington to the bathroom. Gloria and Julia enter from Bedroom 1

Julia It's not looking too hopeful.
Gloria No, it's difficult with an odd number. I'm certainly not going to do it three nights in a row. It will ruin my hands.
Julia Couldn't you wear rubber gloves?
Gloria No, I couldn't. You'll have to do it instead.
Julia No, I can't. I'm no good at washing up. I'm always breaking things.
Gloria What about washing?
Julia Oh, I do that night and morning.
Gloria No, clothes and things.
Julia I've always used next door's washing machine. He loves showing it to people.
Gloria How are you in the kitchen?
Julia About the same as anywhere else.
Gloria Cooking.
Julia Oh, not so good at that.
Gloria Is there anything you can do?
Julia Now let me think . . .
Gloria Are you sure you'll manage it?
Julia I know. I'm very good at dusting.

Gloria So your contribution to the housework will be putting the washing in next door's machine, and dusting.
Julia If only we had someone else to help.
Gloria Someone who'd iron, cook, clean and not complain.
Julia You haven't said what you'll be doing.
Gloria I'll take on the hardest job, the one that needs all the effort and organization—I'll supervise.
Julia Oh, that's very good of you—just a minute I'm not sure that's very fair . . .
Gloria Doesn't Mike do anything to help?
Julia No, he always said that he would leave everything to me as he was sure that I wouldn't want him to interfere. Wasn't that nice of him?
Gloria Oh very! But how did you manage?
Julia Very badly. My cooking did improve once I'd got the hang of the tin-opener.

The doorbell rings. Julia opens the door

Miss Plankton enters

Julia Oh, come in, Miss Plankton. Did you want to see Humbert?
Miss Plankton Well, I certainly didn't want to see you two.
Julia What have we done?
Miss Plankton You've ruined my life that's what you've done.
Gloria How have we done that?
Miss Plankton You've stolen my boy-friend.
Julia Mike's not your boy-friend—he's ours.
Miss Plankton Of course he is. But Humbert's mine, or he was—and now he's yours.
Gloria Oh, you're not worrying about last night, are you?
Miss Plankton No, it's the future that worries me.
Gloria We don't really like Humbert. We were only pretending so Mike's mother wouldn't know we were living here with him.
Miss Plankton You're living here with Humbert?
Gloria No, with Michael. We don't like Humbert.
Miss Plankton You really don't like Humbert?
Gloria No way. He's revolting.
Julia Absolutely awful.
Gloria I wouldn't give him a second look.
Julia I wouldn't give him a first one.
Gloria He's so ugly.
Julia And he dresses so badly.
Gloria And his hair style!
Julia He hasn't got a clue.
Miss Plankton Oh ladies, how kind of you to say so. That's wonderful! I thought I had some serious competition, and now I find he's all mine.
Gloria You don't mean you still fancy him?
Miss Plankton Oh yes, I do—but I don't think he likes me very much. If he's not showing me his little Bertie, it's his new washing machine.
Julia What is it you want him to show you?

Act II

Miss Plankton Affection.
Gloria Doesn't he ever say anything nice to you?
Miss Plankton Never.
Julia Do you give him any encouragement?
Miss Plankton Oh yes, all the time. I said the other day, "Humbert, do you like my new dress?" and he said, "I don't know, what's it like?", and I was wearing it at the time.
Gloria What was it like?
Miss Plankton It was most attractive. It was red with orange and green spots on it.
Julia And he didn't notice that?
Miss Plankton No.
Julia He must be colour blind.
Miss Plankton But, you see, I don't know what I can do to make him notice me.
Gloria If he didn't notice you in that I should give up.
Miss Plankton You mean it was too bright?
Gloria Much too bright. I think you'd do better to wear softer colours.
Miss Plankton I'm afraid I haven't much idea about clothes.
Julia And don't you think you'd be better with a different hair style?
Miss Plankton But I've had this one for twenty years.
Gloria Then it must be time for a change.
Miss Plankton But I wouldn't know what to do, and I don't know whether Humbert would like it.
Julia Does he like it now?
Miss Plankton I don't know. He's never said.
Gloria Have you tried wearing make-up?
Miss Plankton Never.
Gloria I think you should start.
Miss Plankton But I wouldn't know how to, and besides, I haven't got any make-up.
Gloria What do you think, Julia?
Julia Nothing most of the time.
Gloria About Miss Plankton?
Julia I think she could make a lot more of herself.
Miss Plankton But I don't know how to. I haven't any idea what I should do.
Gloria I have.
Miss Plankton You have?
Gloria Yes, I think you should put yourself in our capable hands and we'll transform you.
Miss Plankton But I couldn't. I've always been like this.
Gloria Then it's time you were something else.
Julia Come on, Priscilla, we'll make Humbert sit up and take notice.
Miss Plankton Well, if you're sure.
Julia Couldn't be more certain.
Miss Plankton But what if he doesn't like it?
Gloria Then we'll try something else.

Miss Plankton Very well ladies but nothing too daring.
Gloria As if we would.

Gloria, Julia and Miss Plankton exit to Bedroom 1. Elizabeth enters from Bedroom 2, goes to the bathroom door and rattles the handle

Elizabeth Oh bother.
Mr Carpington (*inside the bathroom, rattling the door*) Help me, please help me someone, I've got locked in.
Elizabeth Who is that in there?
Mr Carpington (*off*) Me.
Elizabeth Me who?
Mr Carpington (*off*) Me, Humbert.
Elizabeth What are you doing in there?
Mr Carpington (*off*) I've got locked in.
Elizabeth Push the bolt back.
Mr Carpington (*off*) I can't.
Elizabeth Try man.
Mr Carpington (*off*) I can't.
Elizabeth Try harder.
Mr Carpington (*off*) I can't.
Elizabeth Why can't you?
Mr Carpington (*off*) There isn't a bolt. It's an automatic lock, but I can't turn the knob.
Elizabeth Of course you can. Try.
Mr Carpington (*off*) I can't.
Elizabeth Try harder.
Mr Carpington (*off*) I can't.
Elizabeth Why can't you?
Mr Carpington (*off*) It's fallen off.
Elizabeth Well, I don't know how to get you out. I'll fetch Henry. (*She goes to Bedroom 2 and opens the door*) Henry come here at once. I need you.

Henry enters

Henry Yes, dear.
Elizabeth I want to get into the bathroom.
Henry Well, I'm not stopping you.
Elizabeth No, you're not, but Humbert is.
Henry Humbert is?
Elizabeth Yes, will you please do something about it.
Henry About it?
Elizabeth Henry, will you open that door.
Henry That door?
Elizabeth Yes, that door.
Henry Oh, yes, dear. (*He goes to the bathroom door and tries it*) I can't open it—it's locked.
Elizabeth Yes, I know it's locked. I want it unlocked.
Henry But there's probably someone in there.

Act II

Elizabeth Of course there is. Humbert's in there.
Henry (*knocking on the door*) Humbert, could you unlock the door?
Mr Carpington (*off*) I can't.
Henry Well, try.
Mr Carpington (*off*) I can't.
Henry Well, try harder.
Mr Carpington (*off*) I can't.
Henry Why not?
Mr Carpington (*off*) Because I've got the knob in my hand. It's fallen off.
Elizabeth Henry, will you get Humbert out of there. I want to get in.
Henry How shall I do it?
Elizabeth Surely I don't have to think of everything for you. It must be very simple to unlock a door.
Henry Yes, it is, dear. Could I have my Barclaycard?
Elizabeth No, Henry, you could not. You know what happened last time I gave it to you. You went and bought a new shirt. I had to take it back and change it didn't I? I didn't like it.
Henry Yes, dear, I know but I want it for . . .
Elizabeth Henry, I told you at the time you were not having it again until you learned to be more careful and bought things I approved of.
Henry Elizabeth, I want that card for . . .
Mr Carpington (*off*) Help me, somebody, please help me.
Elizabeth Henry, will you please stop worrying about your selfish whims, and help Humbert.
Henry I can't help until I get my card.
Elizabeth What do you want it for? There's nothing here that you can pay for with a Barclaycard.
Mr Carpington (*off*) Help me, please help me.
Henry Give me my card and I'll help him.
Elizabeth Oh, very well, if it's the only way to get into the bathroom. Here's the beastly thing.

Henry takes the card and opens the door with it

Henry Come on, Humbert. You'll be all right now.

Mr Carpington enters from the bathroom

Mr Carpington How clever you are. How did you do it?
Henry With this card. I've seen it done on television.
Elizabeth Henry, we don't wish to know what you've seen on television.
Mr Carpington Oh, I must get one of those in case I get stuck again. I never knew you could buy a gadget for opening doors.
Elizabeth Well, now you're out—I'm going in. Henry you go and finish packing.

Elizabeth exits to the bathroom

Henry stands with the card in his hand, looking thoughtful

Henry Yes, dear.
Mr Carpington Where can I finish my studying?

Henry In my room, if you like.
Mr Carpington Thank you very much.
Henry Is it important?
Mr Carpington Oh vital.
Henry When do you get the results?
Mr Carpington As soon as I've asked her, hopefully.
Henry Will she tell you straight away?
Mr Carpington I don't know. They usually say they'll think about it.
Henry What is it you're going in for?
Mr Carpington Marriage, of course.
Henry I didn't know you had to take an examination for that.
Mr Carpington Neither did I, but if it's difficult I won't pass.
Henry But you said you were studying for it.
Mr Carpington Oh no, not for that. I'm studying for the first part.
Henry It's in two parts?
Mr Carpington Oh yes, she has to say yes before I can continue.
Henry But what do you do in the second part?
Mr Carpington Mr Feather, if you need any tuition I would suggest you find your own teacher. Now I must get on with my studying.

Mr Carpington exits to Bedroom 2

Henry is left very puzzled

Miss Plankton enters from Bedroom 1. She is transformed—different hairstyle, low-cut top, etc.

Miss Plankton (*in a sexy voice*) Hallo.
Henry Hallo.
Miss Plankton It's lovely to see you again.
Henry Again?
Miss Plankton What do you think of me now?
Henry You mean I've thought of you before?
Miss Plankton Haven't you?
Henry Thought of you?
Miss Plankton Yes, last night. What did you think last night?
Henry I couldn't tell a lady.
Miss Plankton Of me?
Henry I don't remember you from last night. Surely you weren't one of—we didn't—I mean. . . .
Miss Plankton You don't recognize me?
Henry My dear lady, if I'd seen those before—I mean you before—I would have remembered.
Miss Plankton I knew it—a total transformation.
Henry But who are you?
Miss Plankton I came in thinking there was a party going on.
Henry Oh, there is.
Miss Plankton What now?
Henry Yes. Would you like to come?
Miss Plankton Oh yes. I've never been to a party in the morning before.

Act II

Henry Oh, it's much better—it lasts longer.
Miss Plankton Where is it being held?
Henry In here. (*He opens the door of Bedroom 2*)

Mr Carpington enters

Mr Carpington But I'm trying to do my studying.
Miss Plankton Humbert! What are you doing at this party?
Mr Carpington Party? I've been occupied with studying.
Miss Plankton What, may I ask?
Mr Carpington No, you may not. What are you doing with Mr Feather?
Miss Plankton I am going to a party.
Mr Carpington At ten o'clock in the morning. Are you mad?
Miss Plankton Mr Feather—tell him about the party.
Henry Well, I was trying to make up to this lady—
Mr Carpington That much is obvious.
Henry —for last night.
Mr Carpington What have you to make up for?
Henry Lost time.
Mr Carpington Mr Feather, if you don't unhand Miss Plankton I shall do something unpleasant.
Henry You—you wouldn't insult me?
Mr Carpington No, worse than that.
Henry You'd hit me?
Mr Carpington No, much worse than that.
Henry You'd shoot me?
Mr Carpington No, Mr Feather, I shall call your wife.
Henry O.K. you win.

Henry exits to Bedroom 2

Mr Carpington Now Priscilla, I want to talk to you.
Miss Plankton Oh, do you?
Mr Carpington Yes, I've something to tell you.
Miss Plankton Is it about me? Have you noticed anything?
Mr Carpington No, how could I? I've been locked in the bathroom.
Miss Plankton Please tell me. What do you think?
Mr Carpington It's a very upsetting experience.
Miss Plankton You don't like it!
Mr Carpington No-one could like it.
Miss Plankton None of it?
Mr Carpington Well, I felt quite calm at first, but when I realized it might be for ever I started to feel quite excited in a nervous sort of way.
Miss Plankton You feel quite excited?
Mr Carpington Oh no. Not now it's over.
Miss Plankton It's over? You mean it. It's really over?
Mr Carpington Of course it's over. It was over as soon as Henry used his ingenious gadget.
Miss Plankton He did nothing of the kind.
Mr Carpington Oh yes, he did. He released me from my temporary prison.

Miss Plankton Humbert, are you talking about my appearance?
Mr Carpington No, about my experience in the bathroom.
Miss Plankton Humbert, will you look at me?
Mr Carpington Yes, Priscilla, I am looking.
Miss Plankton Well, what do you think?
Mr Carpington I think that you should wear a vest or you'll catch cold.
Miss Plankton A vest! Is that all you can say? After all my trouble you tell me to wear a vest. Humbert Carpington, I hate you and I hope I never have to set eyes on you again.
Mr Carpington Priscilla, please listen to me.
Miss Plankton Listen to you? Why should I? You're a cold fish and if you think I would have anything to do with you again, you're very much mistaken. I hope you drop dead.
Mr Carpington Priscilla, please hear me out. I've got something to ask you.
Miss Plankton Ask me—what can you have to ask me?
Mr Carpington Priscilla, you know some time ago I asked you if you would do me the honour of looking at my washing machine.
Miss Plankton Yes.
Mr Carpington Well, would you do me the honour of—looking at it again?
Miss Plankton No, I would not, and if that's all you have to say to me, I'm going.
Mr Carpington No, please don't go. That's not really what I wanted.
Miss Plankton I'm waiting.
Mr Carpington Er—Priscilla. You know what I think about you . . .
Miss Plankton Yes, you think I should wear a vest.
Mr Carpington Please, Priscilla, you've got to help me.
Miss Plankton What is it you want me to help you with?
Mr Carpington Could you, would you find it in your heart to help me move my cooker. I want to clean behind it.
Miss Plankton How dare you ask me to clean your cooker! As if I didn't have enough to do cleaning my own.
Mr Carpington Priscilla, could you—er—could you look after Tommy the tarantula while I go on holiday?
Miss Plankton No, I couldn't and I've just about heard enough of your nonsense. You stupid man, you've kept me waiting here all this time, and for what? Absolutely nothing.
Mr Carpington Sit down, Priscilla. I'll try and do better. Just a minute and I'll be back. (*He goes to one side and consults his notes then comes back and peers into her eyes*)
Miss Plankton Humbert, just what do you think you're doing?
Mr Carpington Priscilla, what beautiful grey or green eyes you have.
Miss Plankton They're blue. You are colour blind.
Mr Carpington You should have said "Thank you very much."
Miss Plankton Why should I?
Mr Carpington Because it would have helped.
Miss Plankton In that case. Thank you very much.
Mr Carpington I must say it. I must say it—you have beautiful hair.

Act II

Miss Plankton Have I?
Mr Carpington I don't know, but I must say it.
Miss Plankton But you have said it.
Mr Carpington Just wait there a minute (*He goes into a corner and consults his notebook*) In fact, you are beautiful in the altogether.
Miss Plankton Humbert, how dare you!
Mr Carpington I mean you are altogether beautiful.
Miss Plankton Are you feeling well? Your hands are very hot.
Mr Carpington They are also very pretty and I must kiss them.
Miss Plankton Your hands?
Mr Carpington No, your hands.
Miss Plankton Humbert, I really think I had better go.
Mr Carpington Oh no, please don't—I'm better at the next bit.
Miss Plankton What bit?
Mr Carpington Priscilla, I can't think about anything—
Miss Plankton That much is obvious.
Mr Carpington —but you.
Miss Plankton But you what?
Mr Carpington But you must stop interrupting. I keep losing my place. Wait there a minute. (*He goes into a corner and looks at his book*)
Miss Plankton Humbert, I've had enough. I'm a patient woman but my patience has just run out. You're a fool and an idiot. Just what you're up to I don't know, but I'm going now, and you can do whatever you damn well please. I hope I never see you or hear from you again. You pathetic creep, you ridiculous reptile, you . . .
Mr Carpington Priscilla, will you marry me?
Miss Plankton Oh yes, Humbert. What a wonderful man you are!
Mr Carpington Oh Priscilla.
Miss Plankton Oh, Humbert.
Mr Carpington Oh, Priscilla.
Miss Plankton Oh, Humbert.
Mr Carpington We must get married at once and move away from this area.
Miss Plankton Oh yes, we're not living next door. Far too much temptation comes in and out of this flat.
Mr Carpington There's just one thing that puzzles, me Priscilla. What were you doing here last night?
Miss Plankton Oh—er—er—I came to see Michael.
Mr Carpington Why did you?
Miss Plankton You'll think me very silly.
Mr Carpington My dear Priscilla, of course I won't. How could you ever be silly?
Miss Plankton Well, I'm afraid I was. You see, I've watched Michael for a long time and he seems to be so successful with his romances that I thought he could give me some tuition.
Mr Carpington Oh, you are silly! Who needs tuition. I managed quite well without it.
Miss Plankton Did you, Humbert?

Mr Carpington Of course I did. Look how I swept you off your feet when I proposed.
Miss Plankton No, you didn't Humbert—I was sitting down at the time.
Mr Carpington But you accepted.
Miss Plankton Yes, it's the best offer you've ever made me.
Mr Carpington What do you mean?
Miss Plankton I mean it was better than looking at your washing machine, surpassed cleaning your cooker and was infinitely preferable to looking after your tarantula.
Mr Carpington Oh, I've been rather silly, too.
Miss Plankton Yes, Humbert, you have. But now we've got to the point at last, I suggest we return to your flat and start to make all necessary arrangements.
Mr Carpington Yes, Priscilla.
Miss Plankton The first thing we must do is telephone the London Zoo and see if they have an available cage.
Mr Carpington A cage?
Miss Plankton Yes, Humbert, that tarantula is to go. You, I can stand living with, but the tarantula—*no*!
Mr Carpington But, Priscilla, I like . . .
Miss Plankton No "buts", Humbert, Come along.
Mr Carpington Yes, dear.

Mike and Marion enter from the kitchen

Mike Oh leaving so soon! Can't I tempt you to spend another night with us?
Mr Carpington Young man, you can't tempt me at all. Give my regards to Miss Leyton, though.
Miss Plankton Humbert. come along.
Mr Carpington Yes, dear.

Miss Plankton and Mr Carpington exit out of the front door

Marion I think you're going insane, Mike.
Mike I wouldn't be at all surprised.
Marion Why would I be interested in a beetle buried amongst the begonias in your window box?
Mike Ah, I thought you might want to pay tribute to poor Bertie.
Marion Well, I don't.
Mike Now then do come along to the bathroom and see the new rug. I particularly like the shade of . . .
Marion Mike, will you stop this. Why are you trying to keep me out of the bedroom. Who has Dick got in there with him?
Mike I told you—the doctor.
Marion I don't believe you. I'm going to see for myself.

There is a rattling from the bathroom

Elizabeth Help me! Please help me! I can't get out.
Mike What's the matter, Mother?

Act II

Elizabeth (*off*) I'm locked in.
Mike Oh, I am sorry. Can I help at all?
Elizabeth (*off*) Of course you can—GET ME OUT!
Mike It's only a matter of turning the knob.
Elizabeth (*off*) I know that, you stupid boy, but I can't turn it.
Mike Try, Mother.
Elizabeth (*off*) I can't.
Mike Harder, Mother.
Elizabeth (*off*) I cannot turn this knob.
Mike Why not?
Elizabeth (*off*) Because it's fallen off.
Mike Oh well, I'd better get a screwdriver.
Elizabeth (*off*) A credit card will do it.
Mike It's all right, I've got plenty of change.
Elizabeth (*off*) No, you fool, you can open this type of door with a credit card.
Mike How do you know?
Elizabeth (*off*) Henry's used one to do it.
Mike You've actually locked him out. That's dreadful.
Elizabeth (*off*) Mike—please open this door.
Marion Go on, Mike. You don't want her to have hysterics.
Mike Have you got a credit card?
Marion Oh yes, lots of them.
Mike No wonder Dick's hard up.
Marion Dick wouldn't be hard up if he was more careful.
Mike Or you were.
Elizabeth (*off*) Will you get me out of here?
Marion (*giving him a card*) There you are.

Mike goes to the door and is about to open it

Mike Mother, how did Dad know how to open a door like this.
Elizabeth (*off*) He'd seen it on the television.
Mike He says you won't let him have his television any more . . .
Elizabeth (*off*) Certainly not. He watches the most unsuitable programmes.
Mike He gets a lot of pleasure from it and a lot of good ideas.
Elizabeth (*off*) That's just the trouble.
Mike If you don't let him have his television—I won't let you out.
Elizabeth (*off*) How dare you blackmail me. Let me out at once.
Mike No. I'm going out now. 'Bye.

Elizabeth hammers on the door, then stops

Elizabeth (*off*) Very well, I shall stay in here. Sooner or later you'll have to let me out.
Mike Can he keep his television?
Elizabeth (*off*) No, he cannot.
Mike Now, let me see. Who is it you play bridge with? Ah yes, Cynthia Cunningham. What's her phone number? Look it up will you. Marion?
Elizabeth (*off*) What do you want her phone number for?

Mike Oh, I thought we might have a little chat about the difference between forty-five and fifty-five.
Elizabeth (*off*) Michael, you wouldn't.
Mike Of course I wouldn't. In the same way you wouldn't deprive Dad of his television.
Elizabeth (*off*) Oh, very well.

Mike opens the door of the bathroom

Elizabeth enters

Michael, I want to talk to you about your unscrupulous methods of . . .

Henry enters from Bedroom 2

Where have you been? I needed you.
Henry You did?
Elizabeth Yes, I have been locked in the bathroom, and your dreadful son wouldn't let me out before I'd promised to let you keep your television set.
Henry Oh thank you, Michael. I can really keep it?
Elizabeth Yes, but I shall choose the programmes you will watch.
Henry Yes, dear, but I can still watch Blue . . .
Mike Films?
Henry No. *Blue Peter*. I never miss it.
Elizabeth Ah, Marion I want a word with you too.
Marion Well, make it quick. I want to see what Dick's up to.
Elizabeth Richard is hurt badly and I don't think he'll be up to anything for a long time. I hope you'll give him the care and attention he needs. I would suggest that you start behaving like a wife should instead of hanging about his brother the entire time.
Marion In that case perhaps you would tell your dear son to spend more time with his wife instead of hanging about with his next-door neighbour the entire time.
Elizabeth Next-door neighbour? What do you mean?
Marion That's how all this started. I found him with our next-door neighbour.
Elizabeth So! You really shouldn't be so suspicious. Some jealousy is natural, but this is going too far. I often have a cup of coffee and a chat with my next-door neighbour but Henry is never jealous. Are you, Henry?
Henry (*wearily*) Yes, dear.
Elizabeth Henry!
Henry No, dear?
Elizabeth So I can see absolutely no reason for you to mind Richard being friendly with his neighbour.
Marion Oh, can't you. What does your neighbour look like?
Elizabeth Oh, Herbert's a perfectly ordinary looking man in his sixties.
Marion Well, my neighbour is stunning looking in her twenties.
Elizabeth Oh, but even so there is nothing to indicate that Richard has been taking any more than a friendly interest. After all, I go in to see

Act II

Herbert once a week to make sure he's managing on his own. I often have to rearrange things for him and then we sit down and I tell him how everything should be done properly. He so looks forward to my visits.

Marion Has he taken you upstairs to see his continental quilt?
Elizabeth Of course he hasn't. I don't approve of such things. These new ideas don't appeal to me. Give me good old-fashioned bed-clothes, well-tucked in at the edges. But just a minute, why did you ask me about Herbert's continental quilt? Have you seen it?
Marion Of course not. I don't even know if he's got one.
Elizabeth Well, if he has—he's never shown it to me.
Marion Well, Dick has got one, and he has shown it to our neighbour
Elizabeth You mean . . .
Marion Yes, I found them with it over them.
Elizabeth Oh . . .
Marion Mike's been trying to help me make it up with Dick, but now I think he's trying to help Dick make it with someone else.
Elizabeth This next-door neighbour. What's her name?
Marion Angela Leyton, and she hasn't left him alone since the day we moved in.
Elizabeth She wouldn't be a doctor, by any chance?
Marion A doctor! Don't make me laugh. She hasn't got any brains. A doctor indeed. She works in the local beauty parlour as a masseuse.
Elizabeth Oh dear—not a doctor. (*She looks at Bedroom 3*)
Marion She's in there with him isn't she?
Elizabeth Well . . .
Henry Don't worry, if she's a masseuse she might be doing him a bit of good.
Marion I know what kind of good she'll be doing him. Michael you knew about this, didn't you. You're a deceitful wretch.
Elizabeth Michael, what have you been up to now? I might have known it was all your fault.
Mike Me! How can it possibly be my fault?
Elizabeth I never thought you should live on your own. You've got no sense of responsibility.
Mike Live on my own! I like that! I had to sleep on the sofa. All other accommodation was taken.
Elizabeth You always led him astray as a little boy.
Mike I did not. It was Monica whats-her-name that did that . . .
Marion I'm going in and I'm going to tell that—that . . . husband stealer exactly what I think of her.

Marion exits to Bedroom 3

A violent row is heard

Elizabeth Michael, I'm thoroughly confused as to who is to blame for this but perhaps you would be good enough to work it out for me and inform me, so I'll know which of you I will have to cut out of Henry's will.
Mike Oh yes, Mother, I will—but I'm sure you'll find it has all been

Humbert's fault. After all he was the one who brought his beetle in here and upset you so much.
Elizabeth Yes, Michael, you are right.
Mike And it was his girl-friends who took up an entire bedroom last night.
Elizabeth Any man who has three girl-friends must be a trouble-maker.
Mike And he keeps a tarantula in his bathroom.
Elizabeth Henry, I insist we go straight to Mr Carpington's flat. I want you to give him a piece of my mind.
Henry Couldn't we go home?
Elizabeth No, Henry, we could not. Michael, you must move from this flat at once. I will not have you living next door to that dreadful man. He's setting you a very bad example.
Mike Yes, Mother, but I am strong enough to withstand temptation.
Elizabeth There you are, Henry. What did I tell you? An exemplary life. Takes after me, of course.
Henry Yes, dear.
Elizabeth I hope I shall never hear you doubting your son again.
Henry But it was you who said.
Elizabeth Henry, are you contradicting me?
Henry Yes I am. It was you who thought Michael . . .
Elizabeth Henry! Do you want that television set?
Henry Yes, dear.
Elizabeth Come along, then. Good-bye, Michael. Thank you for putting us up.
Mike It's been a pleasure putting up with you. I mean putting you up.
Henry 'Bye, Mike. Sorry if we interrupted anything.
Mike Don't worry. Normal service will be resumed as soon as possible.
Henry Lucky hound.
Elizabeth What did you say, Henry?
Henry I didn't make a sound.

Henry and Elizabeth exit out of the front door. Dick and Marion enter from Bedroom 2

Dick We're going home now.
Mike Are you sure you can remember the way?
Marion I'm sorry if we've caused you any trouble.
Mike Trouble—what trouble?
Marion 'Bye, Mike.

Marion kisses Mike and exits out of the front door

Dick tries to follow but Mike intercepts him

Mike Well?
Dick Oh, yes. Very well. I took your advice. I used your bedroom this time.
Mike And what about Marion? How did you fix that?
Dick Two words.
Mike Two words?
Dick Fur coat.

Act II

Mike You're learning.

Dick exits out of the front door. Angela enters from Bedroom 3

Angela They're all right. Dick's delighted, Marion's mollified and I'm miserable. I suppose I'll have to move again. I don't think Marion likes me as a neighbour much.
Mike That I can understand.
Angela I don't know where I can go.
Mike It must be a problem.
Angela I suppose you wouldn't like me to move in with you?
Mike That's an offer I've just got to refuse. In that bedroom there are two beautiful young ladies who in a minute I've got to think of a way of pacifying. I think your presence on the scene might make matters a lot worse.
Angela But you do find me attractive?
Mike Of course I do. In fact you're beautiful.
Angela If a vacancy occurred here would you let me know?
Mike You'll be the first on my interview list.
Angela Promise?
Mike Promise.

Angela kisses Mike and exits throught the front door. Julia and Gloria enter from Bedroom 1

Ah, I was just coming to see you two. I expect you're rather angry with me.
Gloria Of course we're not.
Mike You haven't been fighting over me?
Julia Of course we haven't.
Mike Oh.
Gloria Don't sound so disappointed. We've worked it all out.
Mike How clever you are. Who's staying?
Gloria I am.
Julia And I am.
Mike Both of you?
Gloria We knew you'd be pleased.
Mike Oh, very. But I don't see how . . .
Gloria Don't worry. It's all been worked out on a rota system.
Mike What's all been worked out on a rota system?
Julia Everything has. What a busy boy you're going to be.
Gloria Yes, but we do have a small problem . . .
Mike And I've got a large one . . .
Julia Yes, it would work so much better with four.
Mike Four—oh you mean we must find another man.
Gloria No, that's no good. He wouldn't do any housework.
Julia No, we want another girl.
Mike Another girl? Another girl! (*He runs to the front door*) Angela, Angela come back! A vacancy has occurred!

CURTAIN

FURNITURE AND PROPERTY LIST

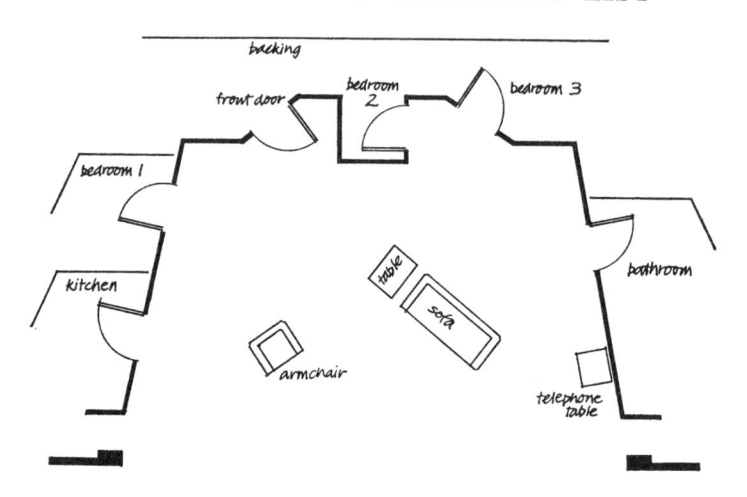

ACT I

On stage: Easy chair. *On it:* cushion
Sofa. *On it:* cushions
Small table
Telephone table. *On it:* telephone, directory
Drinks table. *On it:* 2 bottles of whisky, gin, vodka, brandy, assorted glasses
Carpet

Off stage: 2 pairs of sheets (**Mike**)
Nighties (**Angela, Julia, Gloria**)
Mug of milk (**Elizabeth**)
Mug of milk (**Mike**)

Personal: **Dick:** travelling bag. *In it:* pyjamas
Marion: holdall. *In it:* nightie
Elizabeth: case. *In it:* pyjamas, dressing-gown, sponge-bag
Julia: handbag. *In it:* toothbrush
Henry: case. *In it:* pyjamas
Mr Carpington: matchbox

ACT II

Strike: Dirty glasses

Set: Clean glasses
Cup of coffee **(for Dick)**

Off stage: 2 bottles of milk **(Mike)**
Cup of coffee **(Mike)**
Cup of coffee **(Henry)**
Wig, make-up **(Miss Plankton)**

Personal: **Mr Carpington**: notebook, pencil
Elizabeth: handbag. *In it:* credit card
Marion: handbag. *In it:* credit cards

LIGHTING PLOT

Property fittings required: wall brackets
Interior. An apartment. The same scene throughout

ACT I. Evening

To open: All practicals on

Cue 1	**Mike** switches off lights *All practicals off*	(Page 1)
Cue 2	**Mike** switches on lights *Revert to opening lighting*	(Page 1)

ACT II. Day
To open: General effect of bright summer morning
No cues

EFFECTS PLOT

ACT I

Cue 1	**Mike** moves to Bedroom 3 *Door bell rings*	(Page 1)
Cue 2	**Gloria** and **Dick** exit *Doorbell rings*	(Page 3)
Cue 3	**Mike** downs his drink *Doorbell rings*	(Page 5)
Cue 4	**Mike** exits to bathroom *Doorbell rings*	(Page 6)
Cue 5	**Mike**: "All in the..." *Doorbell rings*	(Page 12)
Cue 6	**Mike** has another drink *Doorbell rings*	(Page 14)
Cue 7	**Mike**: "... it's just not possible." *Doorbell rings*	(Page 15)
Cue 8	**Mike** pushes **Dick** in bedroom after girls *Doorbell rings*	(Page 17)
Cue 9	**Mike**: "I must remember that." *Doorbell rings*	(Page 19)
Cue 10	**Mr Carpington**: "I'm sure I heard something then." *During dialogue party sounds from Bedroom 1*	(Page 23)
Cue 11	**Mike**: "... so I can get to bed." *Crash from Bedroom 1*	(Page 24)
Cue 12	**Elizabeth**: "... when you are anywhere near him." *Doorbell rings*	(Page 25)

ACT II

Cue 13	**Mr Carpington** exits to kitchen *Doorbell rings*	(Page 38)
Cue 14	**Julia**: "... the hang of the tin-opener." *Doorbell rings*	(Page 40)

PRINTED IN GREAT BRITAIN BY
THE LONGDUNN PRESS LTD., BRISTOL.